D0342528

"'Donkeys' carry us through life's challenges and show us how to Stop! Look! and Listen! for God's presence in our circumstances. Virelle fills this delightful book with real-life lessons that bring God's truth alive in application to our everyday lives."

—CAROL KENDALL

director of communications, MOPS International

"Filled with authenticity, humor, truth, and how-tos, *Donkeys Still Talk* reminds us that God's voice can be loud and clear—even when the answers come from unexpected sources."

—CAROL KENT

president, Speak Up Speaker Services;

author of Tame Your Fears

"In a compelling 'aha' way, Virelle Kidder will open your eyes to the many ways God speaks personally to you today. Once you read *Donkeys Still Talk,* you will be looking over your shoulder with a new awareness of God's presence and His great care."

—JAN SILVIOUS

author of Foolproofing Your Life; *conference speaker*

"The book is fabulous! What a blessing Virelle's writing is. She has walked where we walk and knows the paths so well! I couldn't put the book down!"

—JANICE CROUSE

author of Gaining Ground;

coauthor of The Strength of a Godly Woman

"Virelle's seasoned wisdom and heartwarming humor simply make us want to live for Christ. I can't think of better motivation to read a book."

—BRENDA WAGGONER

licensed professional counselor;

author of The Velveteen Woman

"I love this book! I totally identified when Virelle said, 'The stories I most love to tell unfolded on the back of one donkey or another.' Virelle's transparency and candor drew me in and made me want to finish the book in one sitting."

—CAROLE LEWIS

national director, First Place

DONKEYS
STILL TALK

Hearing God's Voice When You're Not Listening

VIRELLE KIDDER

NAVPRESS⊘.

NavPress is the publishing ministry of The Navigators, an international Christian organization and leader in personal spiritual development. NavPress is committed to helping people grow spiritually and enjoy lives of meaning and hope through personal and group resources that are biblically rooted, culturally relevant, and highly practical.

For a free catalog go to www.NavPress.com
or call 1.800.366.7788 in the United States or 1.800.839.4769 in Canada.

ISBN 978-1-57683-460-2

Cover design by David Carlson Design
Cover photo by Veer
Creative Team: Terry Behimer, Traci Mullins, Cara Iverson, Glynese Northam

Some of the anecdotal illustrations in this book are true to life and are included with the permission of the persons involved. All other illustrations are composites of real situations, and any resemblance to people living or dead is coincidental.

Unless otherwise identified, all Scripture quotations in this publication are taken from the HOLY BIBLE: NEW INTERNATIONAL VERSION® (NIV®). Copyright © 1973, 1978, 1984 by International Bible Society. Used by permission of Zondervan Publishing House. All rights reserved. Other versions used include: THE MESSAGE (MSG). Copyright © 1993, 1994, 1995, 1996, 2000, 2001, 2002. Used by permission of NavPress Publishing Group; and the English Standard Version (ESV), copyright © 2001 by Crossway Bibles, a division of Good News Publishers. Used by permission. All rights reserved.

Kidder, Virelle.
  Donkeys still talk : hearing God's voice when you're not listening / Virelle Kidder.
      p. cm.
Includes bibliographical references.
  ISBN 1-57683-460-3 (pbk.)
  1. Christian women--Religious life. 2. Suffering--Religious aspects--Christianity. I. Title.
  BV4527.K473 2004
  248.8'43--dc22
                                        2003019837

Printed in the United States of America
2 3 4 5 6 7 8 9 10 / 12 11 10 09 08

To two forever friends whom I love deeply —

my oldest daughter,
Lauren Elizabeth Kidder McGarry,

and Birgitta Elizabeth Anderson El-Hajj
(October 18, 1967–October 16, 2001).

One is here;
the other was called Home early.

contents

FOReWORD

SISTER, AFTER A couple of decades on the trail with Jesus, I've come to realize that I am one stubborn donkey. Nothing gets in my way like I do! My daily prayer is, "Lord, save me from myself!"

But sometimes the donkeys in our lives are other people or events that appear unexpectedly. We don't throw out a donkey welcome mat or hang a sign in the window that reads, "We speak donkey." Nope. The critters just amble through the door unannounced and start nibbling on the sofa. That's when we need *Donkeys Still Talk*, because that little beastie is there for our benefit and he won't leave until we hear what he has to say.

My girlfriend Virelle is about to help you discover the donkeys in *your* life—problems, challenges, difficult people—and see them for what they are: God getting your attention. Virelle writes from the heart and from experience. Her honesty is refreshing and convicting. Her personal stories invite us to be honest, too: "I'll show you my donkeys; you show me yours."

Here's the truth: When I edit my own manuscripts, I curl up in a comfy chair, pen in hand, and cover the pages with red ink. I did the same with *Donkeys Still Talk*—not because I found any mistakes, but because I kept hearing God's voice whispering to me, "Pay attention, Liz. This one's for you, Liz." Of the many phrases I underlined, this one spoke the loudest: "The soaring freedom we seek is actually found in an unlikely place: obedience."

Hee-haw! Or, more truthfully, *Ouch.*

That's what happens when you read a book by a Christian writer who shoots straight and tells the truth. Obedience is part of that truth, even if we don't want to hear it. No, *especially* if we don't want to hear it.

But Virelle doesn't quit with truth; she presses on to give us hope drawn from her own days of hopelessness. Virelle's list of what she's aiming for in life is so like my own that I suspect it's like yours, too. The first item on the list is, "To be more grateful to God and those around me." *I promise, Lord.* Even if they bray loudly, even if they tromp on my toes, and even if they speak truths I don't want to hear.

I've never learned anything the easy way. If you're at all like me, you'll agree that it's a blessing to have a friend and writer like Virelle Kidder come beside us, tug on our reins, and gently remind us, "Donkeys still talk. Are you ready to listen?"

—LIZ CURTIS HIGGS, best-selling author of
Bad Girls of the Bible and *Thorn in My Heart*

acknowledgments

IT HAD BEEN three years since I'd written a book. With a daily radio show to produce and host as well as plenty of important family needs, I had little time left to write. The problem was, I'm not really happy if I'm not writing. Words, whether spoken or written, are in my blood. And so I prayed one day from the bottom of the dry well, "Lord, do You want me to give up the idea of writing another book?" The prospect was, frankly, depressing.

When I checked my e-mail an hour later, there were inquiries from two publishers. As any writer knows, that was a flat-out miracle. Would I consider writing for them? Would I? One of the e-mails was from Terry Behimer, managing editor at NavPress. We clicked. Over many months, Terry had prayed that my schedule would clear. When I lost my radio show due to financial challenges at our station, I called her the same day. Can I ever thank you enough, Terry? God used you to breathe life back into my writer's heart and give me a dream, riding on a donkey.

Traci Mullins, my "artful crafter," who loves God, the power of words, authors who need lots of coaching like me, dogs, and definitely donkeys: You are the most challenging, encouraging, visionary editor anyone could have. Thank you for putting me back in writing school and "braying" for me regularly!

Lisa Marshall, sharp-as-a-tack NavPress publicist, whom I knew from radio days: Thank you for being the creative link who mentioned me to Terry. I promise to do any media you want me to do.

Thank you, Nicci Jordan, for driving out of your way to buy me the last copy in town of *Traveling Mercies*.

I am forever a Liz Curtis Higgs fan, but not because Liz is funny, although she is beyond funny. And not because Liz is a great writer; she is that, too, and I have devoured every one of her books as soon as it was released. What I love about Liz is that she is the real thing, the authentic article, through and through. She's an honest woman of faith and the writer who best exemplifies for me the dramatic change that can happen in a life that has learned to stop and listen to God. Liz, I feel very honored that you agreed to write the foreword to *Donkeys Still Talk*. I thank you from the bottom of my heart.

Rev. Dr. P. Curtis Morgan, our pastor and dearest friend, along with his wife, Linda: Thank you for being the spiritual filter through which this book passed. You are the best Bible teacher I know, and your words of counsel, prayer, and teaching—as well as many years of loving friendship—have shaped my life.

Bonnie Magill, dear praying friend, exercise buddy, and women's ministry leader: Thank you for combing through the manuscript as a careful reader and a keen listener to God. Your insight has been a valued help.

My fellow writers and speakers in AWSA (Advanced Writers and Speakers Association), particularly Carol Kent and Linda

Evans Shepherd: Thank you for your examples of excellence and integrity, your prayers, and your encouragement.

My dear friends who prayed for me as I wrote (you know who you are) and never saw me: Thank you. Without others praying, writing is impossible. I am deeply grateful that you haven't given up on me yet.

To all the people who allowed me to tell their stories, a very personal thank-you. You added flesh and reality through your willingness to share your life. A special thank-you to Ben and Badger, two adorable donkeys, and their owner, Angie Proper, who opened up their world to me. I am forever a donkey lover!

To Cec Murphey, who has prayed for me many times on his morning run, a big thank-you for your encouragement and great talent over the years. I hope someday I sell as many books as you have!

My dear kids and their spouses and my grandkids, who always love me as "Mom" and "Nana" whether I write anything or not: Thank you for your love and prayers and cheerfulness. What would I ever be without you?

To my loving husband, Steve, "thank you" is not big enough or deep enough. You are hands down the best man on the face of the earth and my greatest friend, soul mate, and encourager. Everything I write about we have learned together. I love you!

And my very patient and loving heavenly Father: Thank You for meeting me in so many unexpected places on this journey. I am sorry I didn't recognize sooner it was You. I'm working on listening better. Thank You for allowing me the thrill of walking with You these many years. I can't wait for what's next.

"IS THAT YOU, GOD?"

I HAD MY "spiritual ears" on early in life. As young as age five or six, I used to talk to God, asking Him to tell me the answers to life. "What's life all about?" I'd whisper in the dark, wondering if anyone could hear. "When I die will I go to heaven? Will my dog be there? And my family?" Serious questions for a little kid. I never heard any answers, but I kept trying.

My favorite place to play was in the dense woods behind our house. (It was safe in those days to let kids build forts and spend most of the day on their own.) My friend Barbie and I wore six-shooters and cowgirl hats and built pretend campfires in our woods or in the fields at her family's farmhouse, imagining we were heroines in the Wild West, another world away. When Barbie couldn't play, I went into the woods alone, pushing back blackberry bushes and following the small path to our hidden fort. On those days, I played with God, talking to Him all day.

When I was seven, my father left. I asked God, "Why?" and "Will you bring my daddy home?" Later, when I was twelve, my daddy died, all alone in another city. By then I had stopped playing in the woods, but I kept asking God, "Where is my daddy now? Is he with You?" God never answered, and eventually I stopped asking.

In fifth grade my teacher, Mrs. Bullock, whom all of us feared and loved at the same time, tapped her long red fingernails on my desk and handed me a sheet of white paper. "Virelle, I want you to enter this writing contest. I think you could win it." Nobody crossed Mrs. Bullock. I wrote my heart out for that contest. The prize was any book you wanted. I had mine all picked out.

I wrote a story complete with chapters and drawings of a boy who lost a horse he loved. The horse, of course, came back in the end. I won the contest, having no idea I was really writing about my father and what I dreamed would happen. As a result of that contest, two things happened that changed my life: Inside me a writer was born, and I brought home my first Bible.

"Why didn't you ask for a storybook, like *Heidi*?" my mother questioned me, looking at the heavy red Bible. How could I explain to her that I wanted to know the answers to life?

"I just wanted a Bible," I mumbled, dashing to my room to open it and begin reading. The first page seemed the place to start. Too hard. Then I found some familiar names: Matthew, Mark, Luke, and John. *They* must have the answers. But nothing made sense. I turned page after page with acute disappointment, finally closing my new Bible and covering it with tears. God had let me down. Like Santa Claus and the Easter Bunny, He must not be real, just a little-girl fantasy.

Fifteen years passed before I began finding my answers. By that time I had married my "dream" husband, Steve, and had a beautiful daughter, Lauren. The year Steve finished graduate school, he took a job at Johns Hopkins University in Baltimore. That July, we moved into a nice rented row house. We had a real salary now, plus a car that worked most of the time. You'd have thought that would have been enough for me. I should have been fulfilled, but something was missing. There was a big hole in my heart that no one understood — not even me.

One day Steve's office mate, Keith, and his wife, Ginny, invited us to church and to their home for dinner. It made us nervous right from the start.

"Let's be nice and go just this once," Steve suggested. "Remember, I work with this guy."

Sitting in church that Sunday, I felt my temples pounding, but not from the Baltimore heat. I was miserably uncomfortable. Could others tell how out of place I felt, that I didn't belong there? Looking around, I felt angry at everyone's smugness — these people seemed so sure they knew the Truth. How could they? It made me angry and yet a little envious. I decided to do some more "research" on my own.

First thing Monday morning I began tearing through the mountain of boxes that remained unpacked in our basement until I found the mildewed Bible I had won in fifth grade. My resolve was simple: I'd read it cover to cover and decide if I could believe it. If it was true and God was who He said He was, then I would give Him my life. (I'd always done everything whole hog.) If not, and God was really just a holiday hoax, I would forget the whole thing and never bother with Him again. I hadn't counted on God eavesdropping on my thoughts.

I sat down on the couch, dusted off the Bible's cover, and opened to the first chapter of Genesis. *Same old story,* I thought, quickly closing it up and heading for the kitchen. Halfway there, another Voice spoke to my heart, ever so softly. Did I imagine it? "Why not read it as if you believed it?"

What's the harm in fifteen more minutes? I thought. So I began to read once again, only this time I couldn't put the book down. It was as if God were turning the pages for me, telling me the story of His children, those who lived well and those who didn't, those who believed and obeyed and those who didn't. It was honest, unembroidered, and to the point. No fluff, no sugary sentiment, no exaggeration. Worst of all, I realized it was the Truth, and nothing for me would ever be the same again. I was hooked.

Life began all over again on that September day when I was twenty-five years old. My family thought I had parked my brains and become a fanatic, but so be it. I never wanted my old life back for a moment. It was two long years before my husband, Steve, shared my faith. On the other hand, our precious four-year-old bowed her head and asked Jesus into her heart only a year after my conversion, and our fellowship together was sweet.

Soon I began to observe something unexpected about God's ways. On several occasions I renewed my initial vow, inviting God, almost begging Him, to have all of me. I didn't realize that would include my time, tears, talents, affections, health (or lack of it), finances (or lack of again), until He began to take them one by one. *Was this,* I questioned, *the way God rewarded His children for their devotion?* He seemed, at times, far too willing to let me hurt, make me wait, or dump me into circumstances that were much too hard. I wondered if I knew Him at all. And that was only the beginning of my journey of faith.

Since that time, hearing God's voice has become an ongoing pursuit for me. Many times, He has seemed frustratingly silent, as though the more I asked Him to speak, the more He turned His back. Other times, He has floated me with ease to the next stop on a stream of good gifts and answered prayers. *Why the inconsistency?* I've wondered. *What is God really after? Is this all a big cosmic game?* I knew I must be missing something.

Life continued to happen, which included four kids, several moves, and much change. Years melted into one another, becoming a kaleidoscope of joys and sorrows, hard work, creativity to make ends meet, and learning to serve God at home, in our neighborhood, and at church. Along with thrilling moments, dramatic answers to prayer, and soaring times of growth came exhaustion, discouragement, and drought. Our spiritual roots extended deeper to take in nourishment, often simply to survive. For years, there appeared to be no relief from the sadness we experienced as a family. Truthfully, some days we wondered if God had forgotten us altogether.

One day a close friend confronted me about how fearful I'd become. Her words hurt, but they were only partly true: Actually, I was terrified. Somewhere in the midst of our difficulties I had stopped trusting God. Little problems had swelled into the bigger problems life is sometimes made of: kids sick enough to be in the hospital; my own health bottoming out regularly, resulting in a dozen surgeries; finances often foreboding with four kids, college bills, and one breadwinner; Steve's mounting job stress. At one time, all four of our children experienced serious chronic health issues ranging from lupus to depression to heart problems and a seizure disorder.

I was haunted by questions: *What would happen to our family? What would God allow next?* I still believed Christ died for my sins and lived in my heart, but the sadness over what He allowed made me wonder how much He really loved me.

It never occurred to me then that God spoke in unexpected places and that the very problems I brought Him in prayer were often intended to carry me to a new listening place, straight into the presence of the God I so earnestly sought. I didn't recognize God's voice in all that happened during those years, but it was there. I didn't see His face as I am beginning to now, or hear His whispered words of encouragement when I was down, or recognize that pointed sense of caution just before I launched a testy zinger at someone. How much I missed! He was always there, waiting to meet me at the street corners of my life to offer direction and comfort me with tender words of love when I badly needed them. How much I missed because I simply wasn't listening or perhaps didn't recognize His voice.

God is speaking to each of us personally all the time—not just to special saints on a mission but to you and me every day of our lives. What an awakening it is to discover that the Author of Life wants us to know His thoughts! Psalm 139 is one of my favorite reality checks when I think God isn't paying attention. Think about what verses 17-18 really mean:

How precious to me are your thoughts, O God!
  How vast is the sum of them!
If I would count them,
  they are more than the sand.
I awake, and I am still with you.
(ESV)

God could have said *clouds in the sky*, but He didn't—He said *sand*. When we came back from the seashore last summer, we had sand *everywhere* for months—in our sneakers, our suitcases, our clothes. Imagine God comparing His thoughts toward us, *each of us individually*, with sand. Does that give you a picture of the sheer volume of those thoughts?

Let's take it down to a smaller scale. Think of your life as an hourglass with sand in it. Picture it as a steady stream of God's thoughts toward you, flowing from the moment you're even conceived in God's mind (better reread all of Psalm 139!) until the day you take your last breath on earth and, if you are His child, enter heaven. What does that picture reveal about God's endless love and concern for you?

There is no special time to listen to God. On His clock the time is always *now*; the date is always *today*. *Yesterday* is just a *today* whose time has lapsed, and *tomorrow* is just another hourglass called *today* waiting for God to turn it upside down. If you're alive, you can be sure God has something to say to you.

Do you know what haunts me? Not that my life is flowing by; I expect that. It's how many of God's personal messages I've missed because I was too busy or not listening or, even worse, cultivating a self-reliant attitude. When it's especially important that God has our full attention, when we've either grown dull in hearing Him or He wants to deliver a very important message we won't miss (hopefully!), He takes more radical measures to orchestrate a face-to-face encounter we never would have expected. Many of these encounters have directed the course of my life. I wouldn't be "me" without them. And, I'm guessing, you wouldn't be "you."

That's what this book is all about: learning to recognize opportunities for encounters with God in everyday life, even when they are least expected or actually welcome, because the very best words He will speak to us personally will come during those times. When God steps out to meet us on our path, it is His agenda that counts, not ours: His plan, His words, His will. It's time to listen with a heart bowed low.

saDDLeD UP anD GOInG nowHeRe

IT BEGAN SO well. A sunny spring morning flooded our living room with promise. With a grand holiday weekend planned, Steve and I kick-started the day, rushing through breakfast and devotions and divvying up the list of tasks to be completed before several of our kids and grandkids showed up later that afternoon. The house was clean; food was in the fridge. We each had just enough time to finish our handful of "must-do's" before everyone arrived.

Although I had long been in the habit of asking for God's blessing on my day, I had little flexibility that day for a real God-encounter. Frankly, it would have been more convenient had He waited until the following week, but I'm learning that God sends His donkeys into my life exactly on schedule whether I'm ready for them or not.

"Hold it right there," you might be saying. "Donkeys? What donkeys?"

Oh, yes—donkeys. Even though they come in disguises, they're as real as you and I. Did I mention that they talk, too? Our donkeys remind us to listen for God's voice, to focus on Jesus, and to trust Him to give us everything we need for the journey. They carry us places we never would have imagined. But I'm getting ahead of myself. Let me take you back to that day a few years ago when a very unwelcome donkey arrived at my door out of nowhere. It messed up everything.

God Knows How to Get Our Attention

It was lunchtime and I had just bolted down a container of strawberry yogurt in the post office parking lot. I remember like it was yesterday looking into the rearview mirror and noticing something was wrong with one side of my face. The signs of paralysis were unmistakable, and I knew instantly either I was having a stroke or this was Bell's palsy again. I called Steve first and then our family doctor. The message from both was insistent: Drive, if you are able, to the doctor's office *now!*

Steve met me there, and within a couple of hours we were both home again, diagnosis and medication in hand, just in time to greet our children.

"Oh, Mom! What happened?" Lauren and Michael folded me together in a long, tight hug. That's when the tears finally came. I'll never forget my eighteen-month-old grandson, Thane, sadly studying my poker face, as if to say, "Why can't you smile, Nana?"

The next morning, more family had arrived, and I looked and felt much worse. While the kids made breakfast and their voices filled the house like yesterday's sunshine, I locked the bathroom door and leaned forward to study myself in the mirror, tears outlining the strangely fallen features on the right side of my face. In its second swipe since my teen years, Bell's palsy jeered at me again, this time with full vengeance. Besides the fact that I looked awful, painful swelling exploded behind my right ear, an exhausting schedule loomed in the weeks and months ahead, and I couldn't speak, smile, or eat without drooling.

Bell's palsy was definitely not on my agenda, but most everything else was. I had prayerfully agreed to a heavy ministry load that spring, closely dovetailing speaking engagements and writing projects that all involved hours of preparation. I was sure God wanted me to do each one. Now this! How did He expect me to do it? Suddenly, I remembered a fellow speaker who once had to do a retreat with no front teeth after the dentist made a mistake fixing her bridge. Humbling didn't begin to cover it. God couldn't possibly want me to speak with a slur and a drool, could He? I don't mind hard work, but humiliation wasn't on my to-do list. Knowing this condition might last months or never even heal at all, I stared into the mirror and groaned at the prospect of looking like this for a long, long time.

Here we go again, I thought. I strained for a sense that God was really with me, that He cared about my life, that He really loved me. Once more I found myself feeling confused because God didn't seem near and the things He allowed seemed hurtful and even unkind. Little did I know that I was about to have another life-altering encounter with the living God.

Is God responsible for every donkey that comes to our door? I'm not sure. Sometimes difficulties, like the wicked insect bite that kept me awake last night, seem to show up just to complicate our lives; they're simply part of living in an imperfect world.

But I am convinced that God can use every donkey that comes our way for a very good purpose: to carry us to a new listening place where we can hear His voice in a life-transforming way.

DON'T PIN THE BLAME ON YOUR DONKEY

Walk back with me in the Old Testament to Numbers 22, where I first became familiar with donkeys that talk.[1]

Balaam was no rocket scientist as a prophet. He set out on a mission he believed God intended, and he was determined to carry it out, even if it became abundantly obvious that God might have had a different plan in mind. (This sounds uncomfortably familiar.) It all began with a big problem, as many encounters with God do. Here is the greatly abbreviated "Virelle's Standard Version" of Balaam and the donkey that told him what for.

The Israelites were busy doing exactly what they were supposed to do. While no one was looking, they multiplied like rabbits into a vast, numberless people. Furthermore, with Moses and Aaron leading them, they were on a winning streak, as everyone in their path found out. Balak, the king of Moab, looked out his window one day and couldn't finish his lunch when he saw them. He knew his days were numbered if he could not find a clever way to defeat this mob. And so he did what all sharp kings did in those days: He sent messengers to someone he thought had influence at times like these. Off they went with money in their pockets to find the questionable prophet Balaam.

The message from Balak was simple: "Curse these Israelites for me so I can get them out of my hair! I know everyone you curse is cursed and everyone you bless is blessed." A little flattery was bound to work.

Balaam thought for a moment and told the messengers, "Stay here overnight. I have to ask the Lord."

God appeared to Balaam during the night and asked, "Who are these men with you?" Now, I can't figure out why God had to ask this. Maybe to see if Balaam really knew what was going on. But God's directive was crystal clear: "Do not go with them. You shall not curse these people. They are blessed."

In the morning, Balaam shoved his hands into his empty pockets, looked at the ground, and said to the Moabite messengers, "Go on home. God won't let me go."

Now, kings are not accustomed to taking "no" for an answer, especially when the stakes are as high as their own hides. So Balak raised the incentive and sent princes this time, along with the promise of lots of money. Balaam, perspiring, protested loudly, "No matter how much you offer me, I won't go against what the Lord says! But stay here, and I'll ask anyway."

It would feel like turning down the California lottery. In Balaam's greedy little heart, he must have wanted God to change His mind—just this once. What's one small curse among so many victories? Then came the test.

God spoke once again to Balaam at night. This time the message contained one important change: "Go with them, but do only what I tell you." *Could it be that God was changing His mind?* Balaam must have wondered. *Maybe this will be my lucky break. I can retire, move to the ocean, and be done with all this prophet stress. Just one small curse is all it would take.* The next morning, he saddled his donkey and went with the princes of Moab.

And God was angry—very angry. He waited for Balaam up the road, His sword drawn.

It always seemed unfair to me that God was angry. After all, hadn't He told Balaam to go? Why get mad? The guy was just doing what he was told! It would have been okay for God to be angry if He were like you and me, but God can see the secret thoughts and intentions of the heart. When He looked inside Balaam's heart, He saw something that didn't belong in someone carrying His message. It could have been greed or willfulness or arrogance or self-reliance. God wanted Balaam to get the message that he needed to stop in his tracks before continuing on with his misguided personal agenda, but only the donkey was listening.

When the little beast first saw God in the road, sword drawn, she quickly turned aside. Balaam lost no time whipping her back onto the path. Soon the path became narrower and ran down between two vineyards with a wall on either side. When the donkey looked up and saw the Lord again, she slammed so hard into the wall that Balaam's foot was crushed. He hit her even harder this time.

Let me stop for a moment and ask those of you who would like to grab that whip and smack the daylights out of Balaam for hitting his donkey: Have you ever confronted a big obstacle in your own path and done something similar? Maybe you don't beat your pets or kick your tires, but how about the way most of us behave when things don't go according to our best-laid plans? Too often, long before we look up to see if God is seeking an encounter with us, we've asked everyone we know and contacted every prayer chain across the country to pray against our donkey's behavior. When that doesn't change things, we claim Scripture verses over it, pray harder, rebuke the Devil, put on sackcloth and ashes. If we're honest about our motives, we might find that our "spiritual" responses to problems aren't much different from Balaam's reaction of beating his donkey.

The third time the angel of the Lord appeared, He stood in the path so there was nowhere else to turn. The donkey lay right down under Balaam. That was it! Balaam had put up with this long enough. He took his staff and viciously whacked the donkey one more time.

With that, God gave the donkey a voice. I wish I could have seen Balaam's face! (This part of the story reminds me that God is the original animal lover!)

"What have I done to you that you have hit me these three times?" the donkey brayed loudly. Brilliant Balaam still didn't get it. He answered her like this chat was normal.

"You made a fool out of me!" he screamed, red-faced. "If I had a sword, I would kill you!"

"Have I been in the habit of doing this to you?" the donkey reasoned, pointing her ears ahead on the path, as if to say, "Look up there, stupid!"

"Well, no," replied Balaam as he finally looked from the donkey to the place where the path narrowed. He squinted. *Funny, it looks strangely bright up there,* he thought, shielding his eyes from the penetrating rays. *Was it this bright the last time I was here? I don't think so.*

"Then the LORD opened Balaam's eyes," Scripture tells us, "and he saw the angel of the LORD standing in the road with his sword drawn. So he bowed low and fell facedown" (Numbers 22:31). That is exactly how any of us should be when God meets us on our paths: prone, silent, listening. The Father of Lights, the Eternal I AM, has something to say. Nothing else matters. Balaam, trembling, bowed low in the dust and finally listened to God.

"Why have you beaten your donkey these three times?" God asked Balaam. "I have come here to oppose you because your path is a reckless one before me. The donkey saw me and turned away from me these three times. If she had not turned away, I would certainly have killed you by now, but I would have spared her" (verses 32-33).

Don't you love the fact that God defends the donkey first? In effect, He's saying, "You foolish person, didn't you know this donkey was honoring Me more than you by refusing to do what you wanted? She was the righteous one and you were the real jackass!"

Balaam, shaking in the dust, groveled in fear and admitted, "I have sinned. I didn't know it was You. If You want me to go back, I'll go back."

God's reply was brief and His terms no-nonsense. "Go with the men, but speak only what I tell you." Questionable as Balaam's credentials were, he was on a God-mission now and his life was clearly at stake as much as the Moabites' lives were.

My guess is that when Balaam finally got up from the ground and approached his donkey, he had some big-time apologizing to do before he hoisted himself into her saddle again. When I've been mad at one of my donkeys—whether it was a young husband who didn't yet share my faith, a teenager who was driving me up the wall, or a nagging health issue—my attitude has changed dramatically when God "opened my eyes" like He did Balaam's. If you'd like to know "the rest of the story" (and it's a good one!), including what happens when Balaam finally shows up to meet King Balak of Moab, you can read about it in Numbers, chapters 23–24. It's a page-turner in which God, the real Hero, wins again.

"Speak, Lord — I'm Listening."

Words matter a lot to God. They give life.

When Jesus confronted the Devil in the wilderness, He used these words: "Man does not live on bread alone, but on every word that comes from the mouth of God" (Matthew 4:4). He wasn't kidding. If we miss God's words to us, we miss the life He wants us to lead in this world. We miss His will; we lose our way; we miss intimacy with Him. Those are very big things to miss. And so God, in love, engineers a meeting. He uses the circumstances of our lives to "hem us in, behind and before" (see Psalm 139:5). He sends a donkey that will get our attention and direct us to the life-giving messages God has for us personally.

"What are you trying to tell me, Lord?" I sniffed at the red-nosed, pathetic face staring back at me in the bathroom mirror. "You've got my attention."

Adversity isn't getting any easier, but after thirty years of following Christ, I'm learning where to turn first. Wiping away my tears on the sleeve of my robe, I asked Him point-blank, "What is it You want me to hear?"

If you are a speaker and God paralyzes part of your mouth, it is a safe assumption that He has something to say. Of that I was sure. I was not aware of any unconfessed sin, but then, it's easy to be blind to our own sin, isn't it? I knew the truth was coming.

I continued to stare into the mirror at my lopsided face. I was going nowhere until I heard God speak. I knew He would, but I wasn't sure how or when or through whom. Waiting is what I least like about following God. It's entirely unnatural for someone whose planner is packed full every day.

God certainly doesn't always speak to me so clearly and directly, but I heard a soft whisper in my heart: "Virelle, where are you going?" (Didn't He ask Balaam something similar?)

"Well, I thought I was on Your mission, Lord," I answered.

"That's true, you are," He said. "I have a perfect plan for your life. Why are you fighting with me?"

Fighting? I was fighting? Since when? I felt like I was working my tail off! "Lord, I didn't know I was fighting You! What are You saying to me?"

"I am so glad you asked, Virelle! I was wondering if you would you still praise Me with only half a mouth."

The gentleness of His question fingered softly through the thin threads of vanity still left in this over-fifty frame, separating the troublesome snarls from the rest, the way I used to comb my daughter's long hair at night, removing the worst tangles one hair at a time without hurting her or letting her know how bad they really were. God's question probed my tangled, tired heart, too. Were there limits in my love for Him? Would I be willing to carry His love to others while looking strangely poker-faced and foolish, drooling and garbling words? Would I be His funny-looking messenger, just because He sent me?

"Yes, Lord," I answered reluctantly, knowing I might be saying "yes" to long-term paralysis. But yielding felt good in a way. Trying to maintain control is exhausting.

"Then, Virelle," I heard God whisper, "will you remember that I will never give you more than I equip you to do?" I winced, remembering the mammoth wall calendar in my office filled with daily "must-do's" in tiny print that spoke clearly of my doubt that I could ever complete all God seemed to require of me that year. It was true: I thought it was all up to me. My inner voice said, *Perform, Virelle! Get it done and do it well!* How wrong I was to give God a voice like mine and view Him as just a bigger taskmaster.

My face hot with shame, the doubter whispered back, "Yes, Lord."

"Good! Will you follow Me a little more quietly now?"

The line now drawn would mean no more complaining, no more fussing about the demands I felt in my life, no more making such a big deal about what God had for me to do. God wanted from me the same thing I loved hearing from my kids when I asked them to do something: "Sure, Mom! No problem!" A taller order for me than I realized.

"Yes, Lord," I said. "But just one thing. I can't smile at my husband, my children, my grandchildren. Will I never be able to smile at them again?" Just thinking about it turned on a faucet of tears.

"Then smile at *Me*," He answered gently. "I will always see your smile, and I think it's beautiful."

Sometimes when God speaks, He gives us nothing we ask for and everything we need. It's a whole different ball game feeling convinced, as I began to that day, that God is with me every moment. He's with you, too. He has a good plan, a wonderful plan, and asks only that we trust Him with each day's needs. Big needs bring big provisions; smaller needs, smaller provisions. The serendipity for me that day was the gift of a quieted heart.

The provisions came as promised. Just days before I left on a ministry trip, my speech returned. About eight weeks later, a tingling sensation began first in the corner of my mouth and gradually liberated the rest of my face a little at a time in the weeks that followed. Today, a very mild paralysis remains.

Now I'm even grateful for the little downward curve of my mouth on one side when I'm tired (it lets me know I need to rest) and for my one stationary eyebrow (raising only one looks exotic). Maybe God allowed these physical signs to remind me of our encounter. When He speaks, it's always best to listen. When He directs, it's best to obey. When He corrects, it's in my best interest to change course. And when He tells me something wonderful, it's a good idea to believe Him.

Hearing God's voice and redirecting our lives according to

His plans is always best; it's just not always welcome at the moment. The donkeys that show up come disguised as all sorts of things, such as Bell's palsy or other health challenges, problems in parenting, financial reversals, mothers-in-law (now *there's* a tempting word picture for my kids' spouses!), even a car that won't start. They come in all colors, sizes, and shapes.

My guess is that there are at least a couple of donkeys braying outside your door right now. In the pages ahead, we'll talk about how to identify them, where they come from, why we get so angry and frustrated when they won't budge, and why their messages are more critical than anything on our "must-do" list.

If you're ready for a real God-encounter, saddle up! It's just ahead.[2]

Face to Face

- Begin to record your journey. Each chapter in this book has a Face to Face section with reflection questions; it might be helpful to write your answers in a journal. Does the word journal sound like one more "must-do"? Then rename it! Call it a treasure chest or anything you like where you will keep the most valued words of your life: your honest prayers to God and His personal answers to you. I use a simple composition notebook. In the front I record insights God gives me as I study His Word each day. Sometimes I use that space to list my dreams and goals, and then I pray over them. In the back, starting from the last page and moving toward the middle of my notebook, I name my donkeys as prayer requests and put the date to the left of the request. When God speaks through His Word or circumstances or others' voices, I write the answer and the date in the margin. Over many years, this has proved the best way I know to remember the most treasured workings of God in my life. Try it. You may find a better way that suits you, but begin today, even if it's only with a few words jotted down each morning.

- Now hop in the saddle by reading all of Psalm 139 out loud. Reading familiar words aloud is a great way to add impact. Does a new thought startle you in these verses about the depth of God's concern and love for you? Is there anything about God's personal love for you that you haven't considered before?

• Can you recall a time when a donkey dressed like challenging circumstances changed the course of your life? How so? Did it draw you closer to God, or did you turn your face away from His in bitterness, disillusionment, or anger? List as many of these people or events as you can. Describe any lasting effect on your life or walk with God.

• Does reading Psalm 139 cause you to look at those events differently today? Was there a message you might have missed? Record in your journal the most personal thing you think you hear God saying to you in this psalm. Write it down as if God were speaking to you directly.

• Write a prayer of response to God. If you feel hemmed in today, tell Him why. Then ask Him to speak any way He chooses to your listening heart.

• Sometimes busyness, discord in our relationships, or nagging moral foul-ups become "static" in our lives that interferes with our ability to hear from God. Is there static you need to confess to God right now, asking His forgiveness and help to tune it out?

Truth for the Surefooted Journey

In the beginning was the Word, and the Word was with God, and the Word was God. He was with God in the beginning. Through him all things were made; without him nothing was made that has been made. In him was life, and that life was the light of men. The light shines in the darkness, but the darkness has not understood it. (John 1:1-5)

Speak, [Lord,] for your servant is listening.

(1 Samuel 3:10)

CHAPTER TWO

HEE-HAW! MEET YOUR DONKEY

WE ALL HAVE donkeys in our lives. Seldom cooperative, they are the challenging circumstances we ride from day to day. Your donkey may be a difficult boss, a job loss, a rebellious teenager, or too-tight finances. It may be a health challenge, an emotional issue, or the failure to achieve success in some area of your life. You know your donkey's name. Every time you think of it you are perplexed, irritated, or stressed—perhaps even angry with God over the balky way this donkey is carrying you. It's driven you to higher levels of headache and stomach acid remedies. You've blamed the beast a hundred different ways and tried every possible means to turn it around, but it stays its stubborn course.

The donkeys we ride don't look like fuzzy-eared burros; they often look more like people with big needs and problems that won't budge. Without our spiritual eyes opened, we seldom recognize that God is involved in every detail of this journey called life. He has a perfect plan for our lives, but finding it means listening to Him with a humble heart. Whatever donkey you are riding, expect God to meet you en route.

Name Your Donkeys, Name Them One by One

When I speak to groups and ask women to name their donkeys, invariably there is an uncomfortable silence followed by a few nervous chuckles and then a prolonged period of gut-level honesty. It's common to hear, "My donkey's name is Ron and I'm married to him!" That's always good for a laugh that we all know isn't really funny.

"Mine's my troubled teenage daughter." Audible groans from around the audience bear witness to a shared journey.

"My elderly parents who live with us."

"My boss."

"The board members of my homeowners' association."

"What about the donkeys," I ask, "who aren't people but challenges you face day by day?" Often the question evokes tears.

"Anxiety attacks."

"Clinical depression."

"Loneliness."

"Perfectionism."

"Infertility."

"Bulimia."

"Chronic health problems."

"My husband's unfaithfulness."

Even sadder, "I hate who I am."

Some people have trouble identifying their donkeys. Perhaps you know yours by another name. Like the dog who thought his name was "Go lie down!" your donkey's name may begin with, "If only . . . "

"If only my husband were a believer."

"If only my son (or daughter) didn't have ADD."

"If only I had a job I liked."

"If only we had more money."

"If only I hadn't been abused as a child."

"If only my marriage had worked out."

"If only I wasn't so fat" (or stupid, nervous, tall, short, timid, or whatever negative label comes to mind).

Donkeys can be as simple as blocked plans, a blown radiator hose, or financial drought. But more often than not, they involve people whose lives are intertwined with ours, whose needs create pressures, even heartbreak, on a regular basis.

Still not sure? Eavesdrop on your conversations, especially your prayers. What has you pinned against a wall? What keeps you from feeling free or holds you back from going where you want to go and doing what you want to do? Can you name the thing that discourages you most, frustrates you, maybe even threatens to crush your spirit or break your heart? My guess is that it's a donkey you have grown to dislike intensely and blame for nearly all the limits you feel are imposed on your life. It may symbolize the great disappointment you feel in yourself, in others, and even in God.

If you are feeling upset right now, I have good news: You not only have lots of company but also a big surprise and quite possibly a great deal of joy ahead of you. There's no better place to hear God's voice than on your donkey's back. Why is that? Because the pressing needs we feel in the midst of our trials encourage us to seek God face-to-face, which in turn strips away the fluff that has surrounded our idea of who God is. Donkeys bring us back to basics, to an encounter with God that can literally change our lives. Unfortunately, He usually begins the positive transformation by dealing with the impatient and bewildered rider.

TAMING THE RIDER

It's funny. For much of my life I've moved from one donkey to another, saddling them with the reins of my own agenda firmly in hand, clearly on a mission. When I saw little progress, I would whip each one with my fevered prayers and wear out every friend who would listen, begging her advice on how to budge this burro. Quite honestly, I've often resented the intrusion these donkeys made on my life and thought God unfair to allow my plans and progress to be blocked. Hear the key words: "*my* life," "*my* plans," "*my* progress," "*my, my, my!*" Whether a broken transmission or broken health, these braying obstacles regularly messed up my life and revealed how like Balaam I can be when things go wrong. I remember one donkey that literally moved in with us early in our marriage.

I thought I should have been so happy. Hadn't God answered all my most "impossible" prayers only two years into my Christian life? What more could I want? Steve had finally yielded his heart to Jesus, a miracle many thought would never happen to this young intellectual. Instantly, we had a string of miracles: a new job in the Boston area, a new house purchased without a penny of savings, a wonderful new church family complete with mentors, and a third baby (the son we'd dreamed of). There was one small snag: Steve hated his new job. We all did—even the baby.

You see, Daddy was gone a lot. With Steve hopping a flight every week to another glamorous city, it was becoming a real drag to drum up a "Daddy's coming home!" party every Friday night. Did I mention I was becoming a real drag, too? In between packing and unpacking, doing laundry, and ironing for Steve's next trip (planning for outside help was not my strong suit), I started to feel cooped up, lonely, and miserable. In spite of hopping from one five-star hotel to another, Steve was pretty miserable, too.

One day, Steve leaned back in his office chair, looked down the row of desks at work, and noticed something startling: Everyone in his new company was either single or divorced. *Hmmm,* he thought. *I wonder what's going on here?* Steve knew he needed another job—and soon—if our family was to survive.

That night, after our kids were tucked in bed, Steve unloaded his concern. The solution seemed simple: Change jobs! How hard could that be in the Boston area? There must be thousands of jobs here in Steve's field.

"You can find another job around here, can't you, Steve?" I asked.

"Well, I'll try," he replied tentatively. Of course, God wouldn't move us into a new house complete with a great neighborhood and church only to move us fifteen months later! Of course He wouldn't. And so we prayed together, asking God for exactly what we wanted. I slept peacefully that night, fully expecting another wonderful miracle. The problem was, nothing happened.

Weeks went by; then months. Steve sent out résumés all over the area with no response—except for one crazy, unsolicited job offer in Albany, New York. After spending almost eight years in college and grad school in Albany, neither of us relished a return move. We asked everyone we knew to pray for a new job to open up for Steve near Boston, frequently inviting couples from church over for dinner or dessert, hoping they'd provide just the answer (or job lead) we were looking for—fast! Nothing happened, except that Albany kept calling Steve to come for an interview.

"Promise me you won't take a job there, honey," I pleaded one day. I just couldn't bear giving up the life we had begun in Boston. I wanted us to stay there and blossom. Albany looked colorless and ordinary in comparison.

Steve hugged me and said, "Maybe I should just go to the interview and see what it's about." Reluctantly, I agreed. He left the next day on an early-morning flight.

Shortly after noon, the phone rang. I sat down on our bed to answer it. *Could Steve be done already?* I wondered.

"Hi, honey," he began softly, then paused and cleared his throat. "I know you may not like this, but they've offered me the job. There's a small salary cut involved, but that's okay. It's a better life for our family. I really think this is where God wants me, and I'd like to say 'yes.' Will you come?"

"You're kidding, right?" I asked, knowing the answer. Tears came quickly. I could hardly speak. "Are you sure?"

"Yes, I am," was his quiet reply. Steve never spoke carelessly. I knew he wouldn't ask me to do this if he weren't very sure. *Oh, God, is this how You are answering our prayers?* Apparently it was.

"Then I'll come," I answered, barely able to choke out the words. After Steve finished sharing the dreaded details, I hung up and angrily tossed the phone onto the bed, slumped to the floor, and burst into tears.

"God, this isn't fair! This isn't what we prayed for! Why Albany, Lord? Why do we have to do this? Isn't there anyplace around here where Steve could work?" For almost two hours, I had a major hissy fit, my last-ditch effort to change God's plan. Finally, I just gave up out of sheer frustration. What happened next surprised even me.

I began to overhear myself thanking God again for every miracle gift He had given when we had moved to Boston: the house and the money to buy it, our new church and wonderful friends, the children who came to our house every week for a Bible storytime, our daughter's happy school environment, and especially our great neighbors. Now we had to leave it all. Trembling, I sniffled another prayer: "You can do what You want with us, Lord. If this move is Your idea, I won't fight it any longer." I felt God calling me to trust Him for my whole future, even if it was not what I would have chosen. I didn't feel elated at the idea of surrender, but I did feel a subtle change begin in my heart. I didn't know it at the time, but it wasn't the donkey God was after; it was the rider.

Later that same day, Steve accepted the new job. He called

me again at four o'clock. This time he was standing in my mother's kitchen with a real estate agent. "I found us a house," he said in the same tone he might say, "I'm bringing home dinner."

"You're kidding, right?" I responded. I began to feel hopelessly roped in all over again. *God, are You listening to this? Do I also have to move into a house I've never seen before? You might as well have it Your way, but just so You know: I'm not happy!*

"What color is it?" I asked flatly.

"It's green—light green. It's new and it has four bedrooms. It's a little small, but your mother says it's in the best school district in the area. Do you want me to buy it?"

"Sure, buy it," I answered, with no enthusiasm whatsoever. What difference did a house make now? With God and my mother on Steve's side, I was clearly outnumbered. Of course, God would understand if we built another house in a few years. That seemed a reasonable compromise to me.

I could hear the agent in the background, sending loud whispered messages to Steve to stop right there. She had never sold a house over the phone in her life. I heard her hiss, "Your wife will kill me! She has to see the house first!"

"Oh, no, she's just fine. Virelle says green with four bedrooms is fine. We'll buy it. When can we move in?"

The answer was, way too soon. Three weeks later we were packed and moving from Boston to Albany in a blinding spring blizzard. The usual three-hour trip across the mountains took nearly eight hours, and everyone but Steve had bronchitis. I hadn't been able to talk in two days, which was probably a good thing.

We bunked for the night at my mother's house, coughing all over the place and devouring her famous "get-well soup" until the moving van arrived and backed down our new driveway. Steve unlocked the door to our little green house while I placed a plaque near the doorframe bearing the "fish" symbol and the cross. If God picked out this house, it might as well belong to Him.

It wasn't long before God let me have a small peek at His plans. The next day, our neighbors across the street arrived to greet us. Marilyn later told me, "When I saw that 'fish' symbol, I knew you were the friend I'd prayed God would send." She became a treasured Christian friend within a short time. More blessings followed, including a neighborhood Bible study, wonderful friends for our children (many who came to Christ through them), a truly amazing school district (Mother was right!), and a church family that would pray for us and help shepherd our kids into adulthood.

I wouldn't be telling the truth if I said I lived happily ever after in that house. Even with a large family-room addition and a remodeled kitchen, it always felt cramped. Every spring, model homes called my name. With Steve's blessing, I would scour the area looking for a better place that still felt like home. Alas, I never found one. I'm still here, almost thirty years later. Happier, yes, and much more content. But I still check out the real-estate section in the classifieds now and then, just in case. . . .

WHAT'S GOD AFTER, ANYWAY?

Perhaps you're starting to wonder if God only meets us on the path when He's angry or out to "confront" us. That's not always the case. Very often, He has quite another plan in mind, one we couldn't guess in a thousand years. If your circumstances couldn't look worse to you right now, consider Joseph as a spoiled teenager, sharing with his eleven brothers and father the dreams he had at night that elevated him over his entire household.[1] He never could have conceived at the time that his nighttime fantasies were from God, who had a giant-sized dream for this miracle baby born late in life to Jacob and Rachel. Joseph was clearly his father's favorite, as his custom-made duds advertised. Needless to say, this didn't go over well with his jealous older brothers, who lost no time conveniently "losing" the seventeen-year-old in a ditch one day. They soon sold him into slavery to a greedy band of Ishmaelites headed for Egypt.

Talk about an unwelcome donkey! Captive and probably in chains, young Joseph was as good as dead. But God had a plan for Joseph to prosper in Egypt beyond even this young man's wildest dreams. First, God needed to smooth Joseph's many rough edges and test his character.

The first test was of Joseph's faithfulness. Potiphar, captain of the guard, recognized a good thing in this handsome, brawny lad and bought Joseph from the Ishmaelites for a song. He soon realized the boy was a management whiz and put his entire household under Joseph's thumb—everything, of course, but his wife. Then came the acid test.

One fine day, Potiphar's drop-dead-gorgeous wife could stand it no longer and flung herself at Joseph, tearing off his robe. Most men would have crumpled right there and hopped into the sack with her, but not Joseph. While the humiliated floozy cried "rape!" he left his cloak in her sweaty hands and ran like the wind.

Soon God rewarded Joseph for his integrity with yet another donkey ride: prison, where he was left to rot. Life really isn't fair, is it? After doing everything right, that's what he got. Being the mother of two sons, picturing Joseph in prison breaks my heart. But let's not pass judgment on how fair or unfair God is before we see the entire picture. There's a whole lot more to this story.

Having passed the test of faithfulness under fire, another dreaded test remained: waiting for God to act, which is always a longer and harder test than any of us would like. Joseph no doubt asked himself the same questions we all do: *What if God doesn't do anything? What if He doesn't care what happens to me? What if He leaves me here* (on this donkey) *forever?*

But God did remember Joseph in prison. He looked inside His lionhearted dreamer boy and saw a man who wanted to please Him, no matter what happened. It was time to lift him up.

Maybe that's what God is looking for in our hearts, too: faithfulness under fire, willingness to wait with a quieted, surrendered heart, no matter what happens. Those marks of spiritual maturity are not quickly earned.

God gave Joseph more than a dream; He gave him the ticket to greatness in his ability to interpret others' dreams. Though more discouragement lay ahead when others forgot his help, eventually Joseph's talents were remembered, and he was ushered one bright morning into Pharoah's presence on yet another donkey: Pharoah's own disturbing dreams.

Imagine the stress. One mistake interpreting this puppy could cost him his life! But God gave Joseph the clear interpretation of Pharoah's dream and soon elevated him to an even greater place of power and influence in Egypt, second in command only to Pharoah himself.

Consider the kind of level head and wisdom a job like that would take. Joseph spent a lot of time waiting for God to act, praying for help, surrendering his dreams, committing his heart to God no matter what the outcome. He heard God's voice through his donkeys in the most unexpected places: the pit, the prison, and the palace. He was now perfectly prepared for what God had intended all along: to rescue His people, gather them together in a new home, and to be a blessing to multitudes more in the future.

Do you think Joseph would change any part of his story if he told it today? Would he skip over the bad parts and jump right into his dream of having all his brothers, even the greater known world, bow down to him? I rather doubt it. I think Joseph might give the donkeys he rode some credit for making him into the leader he became. On their backs he learned to bow down, listen to God, and obey Him at every new turn by deciding ahead of time that pleasing God is its own greatest reward. No joy fills the heart more than pleasing God right where you are.

RIDING WITH PURPOSE

Nothing much has changed since Joseph's time. God's purpose is the same for you and me. If you are in the pit right now or feel imprisoned by your problems, nothing gives God more pleasure than speaking to your listening heart. Donkeys are intended to carry us to unexpected places where God's power can be displayed.

There is no shame in riding a donkey. Lots of good folks in the Bible traveled on one. Abraham placed his son Isaac on a donkey and agonized all the way up Mount Moriah, where God asked him to sacrifice his precious child (see Genesis 22). We know now that God powerfully intervened, sparing Isaac, but one day He would not spare His own Son.

Mary, another teenager on a God-mission, probably rode a donkey heading into Bethlehem, carrying Jesus in her womb. There she would deliver the King (see Luke 2:1-7). How blessed was that journey?

Jesus Himself made a public statement when He rode a donkey's foal into Jerusalem on what we now call Palm Sunday. Our King of kings riding on a lowly beast. Only the spiritually blind missed the message (see Matthew 21:1-11).

Do you think Abraham regretted making his journey? How about Mary? Certainly Jesus didn't! How about us? Are we riding our donkeys with remorse over where we are right now, with our head hung down, feeling dejected and forgotten? Or are we carried along by the hope of witnessing and showcasing God's power and faithfulness? God hasn't forgotten us, either.

Have you had dreams about where God might one day carry you? Does it seem like the fulfillment of those dreams is impossible because of where you are right now? Nothing's working out, your life feels like a box with no air in it, no light—like Joseph's prison cell. But maybe the donkeys you are riding are preparing you, as they did Joseph, for the next God-assignment. Ask Him to show you how to live faithfully right where you are, listen for His voice in your own circumstances, and honor Him by waiting with a quiet heart.

Within days after I first invited Christ to take over my unruly, unquiet heart, He began to form a story in me. I'd lie in bed at night looking over the past, noticing for the first time God's fingerprints on my father's life, our family, my playtime in the woods as a little cowgirl talking to God. A thrilling truth began to grow in me: "God loves me! He was there all the time, even though I didn't know it! He's leading me somewhere good."

Being the talker that I am, I felt compelled to tell someone. I dreamed of talking to teenagers, our youth group at church, women's groups, anyone who would listen. But no one asked for my story except my four-year-old daughter. She listened all day and loved it.

It was at least ten years before anyone else asked for my story. By that time I'd ridden a number of donkeys, learning a good deal more about bowing low and listening to God. I had even learned a bit about being quiet. Not much, maybe, but everyone has to start somewhere. When the time finally came to share my story publicly, I was a basket case. But God sent me two angels, named Imy and Ellie, to draw the story out of my heart and teach me how to tell it for the glory of God.

Your life tells a story, too. And the donkeys you ride, just like Joseph's and mine, are an important part of who you are. I know it's hard when we have only a glimmer of light about what God intends. But it is enough simply to follow the light we have, trusting God to illuminate more of the path in time. For today, that is all He asks.

Whatever donkey you are riding, no matter how long it stands there and won't budge, even if it threatens to crush you, one thing is certain: God will meet you in a setting you cannot script. He chooses the time and place, but He *will* come and He *will* speak. What He says will be a story worth telling for a long, long time.

Face to Face

• Try listing your donkeys, naming them one by one. Some you may have grown to appreciate over the years; others are still annoying. Look right into those big brown eyes and fuzzy faces and ask yourself what it is about each one that blocks your path or frustrates you. Could it be that God is speaking through this donkey and you have never quieted yourself enough to hear His voice? Why not turn your face to whatever light there is on your path, bow down, and listen again? Write down what you hear.

• How do you think Joseph's closeness to his earthly father shaped his life? What impresses you most about Joseph?

• Have you ever wondered what impresses God? In his book *The Journey of Desire,* John Eldredge talks about what does *not* impress God: "We hide our true desire and call it maturity. Jesus is not impressed. He points to the less sophisticated attitude of a child as a better way to live. Why are we so embarrassed by our desire? Why do we pretend that we're doing fine, thank you, that we don't need a thing?"[2] Tell yourself and God the truth about the donkeys you are riding today. Tell the truth about why you are troubled about each one. What would you most like God to do about what concerns you?

• Another thing to be truthful with God about is your real dreams and desires. You may feel that your circumstances make them impossible to achieve. I felt like that once, too. I found it liberating to list my dreams and desires in the prayer section of my journal. Telling God the truth for the first time, I saw how He had begun preparing me to realize those dreams since my childhood. Trust the Dream-Giver with a confession of your own desires. Pray for each one, mentally placing it in His hand, and ask God to shepherd that dream into what He desires.

• Psalm 16:5-11 talks about the joys of an obedient life led by God. Is there anywhere you would not go if God moved your "boundary lines"? Do you have an "Albany" somewhere like I did? What would you give up, other than your own way, if you said, "I will" instead of "I won't"? What might you gain?

Truth for the Surefooted Journey

As for God, his way is perfect;
  the word of the LORD is flawless.
He is a shield
  for all who take refuge in him.
(Psalm 18:30)

Trust in the LORD with all your heart
  and lean not on your own understanding;
in all your ways acknowledge him,
  and he will make your paths straight.
(Proverbs 3:5-6)

CHAPTER THREE

HANDING GOD THE REINS

IMAGINE WHAT IT might be like to descend the Grand Canyon on the back of a donkey. First, he is only as tall as you were in fifth grade, if that. Second, the guy looks much too calm for what you are about to do together: descend thousands of feet down one of the steepest canyons in the world on a zigzagging path about three feet wide minus guardrails. Feeling ready yet?

Alternately snorting and laughing at you (that's what a good "hee-haw" bray sounds like), he casts a casual look in your direction while you figure out how to hoist yourself up onto his far-too-small-for-your-fanny saddle. And those big brown Disney eyes and huge comical ears that look like cell phone towers! It's hard to take this beast seriously. Yet this is the animal that holds your life on his shaggy back. Now please drop the reins. He has everything under control.

Although donkeys may seem somewhat passive and vacant mentally, that's not true. They are highly intelligent, calm, sure-footed servants that seldom, if ever, stumble. Naturally sweet-natured and patient, they even make good babysitters. (Why didn't someone tell me that thirty years ago?) Donkeys are even safe for children to ride. By the way, those big ears are safety gear. Like radar, they help donkeys listen for predators. If a coyote or wolf shows up, your donkey will kick it into the next county.

In Bible times, donkeys were more like SUVs without the oversized tires and CD players. Nearly every home had one. You could drive them over all kinds of terrain, hauling the kids plus cargo. Kept in an adjacent stable, they were ready to go at a moment's notice. Donkeys were the original road-hugging 4 x 4s! The difference is, donkeys eat cheap—mostly grass and water—while an SUV will suck your coffers dry.

Best of all, donkeys are trustworthy, loyal servants. And when God sends them on missions, they take their jobs very seriously.

"What If . . . ?"

You may be asking, "So how do I know if my 'donkey' is from God or not?" Sorry, but we don't always know—not at first, anyway. But prayer, along with honest self-examination, gives us a clue.

"What if I brought on this donkey myself?" you might ask. "What if God is punishing me for something?" Start by asking God for discernment, honestly confessing ways you may have barged ahead with selfish plans and made a mess of things. Who hasn't done that? The good news we never outgrow is that He promises to forgive us when we own up to our sins and shortcomings (see 1 John 1:9).

Back to the donkey. The view from Balaam's saddle, and

often ours, is that a donkey on a mission is anything or anyone that brings us to a narrow place in life, hinders our choices, blocks our paths, or in any way frustrates our progress. If you're anything like me, you've ridden a lot of them by now.

It's good to realize that donkeys are not bad in themselves, but they can lead us to difficult choices that involve yielding our will. They show us how much we need God, that life's journey is too dangerous to handle on our own. Donkeys will carry us to places we never planned to go, where we yearn for God to lead us to safety. The rub is, first we must hand Him the reins, which anybody knows is definitely not for sissies. When we do that, anxiety grips us instantly with any number of white-knuckle questions:

• What if God leads me where I don't want to go?
• What if my obedience causes others to suffer?
• What if I have to make amends to someone?
• What if I lose my place in ministry, in my family, in my career?
• What if He leads me to a life I hadn't planned on?
• What if I fail or don't make it?

Life keeps happening, doesn't it? Each day brings decisions to make, changes in plans, surprises both good and bad. Whether you are getting married, are taking on a new job, or have just been laid off, every bend in the road brings both opportunity and risk. Sometimes it feels scary to say "yes" to God, to invite Him to lead. The trouble is, when we don't, the "what-ifs" can halt our progress altogether.

Remember the first time you learned to float? I remember my first time vividly. *I know the water is supposed to hold me up, but will it? I mean, what if it fails me? Other very nice people have drowned; why not me?* I asked myself those questions for thirty-five years in the shallow end of the pool until I finally learned to swim in a Red Cross adult swim program. Even now it amazes me that I not only learned but also went on to teach swimming to other terrified adults. For me, getting my certification as a water safety instructor felt equivalent to getting a Ph.D.

Handing God the reins is like learning to float without your life vest. Little by little, you lie back and take a breath. You're not dead yet. You even feel good, a little giddy, free. Then some wave of fear washes over your face, and down you go. What happened? Did God let go?

Actually, life happened. With each new alarm, we reach for control again, like trying to touch bottom. *What's the matter, God? Didn't You see that wave coming? Maybe I'd better take over now! You weren't paying attention!*

Why are we like that? Why am *I?* I can think of several reasons without even trying hard — pride, for example. *I can handle this myself, thank You!* Flashing on my mental screen is a snapshot of my pride literally taking a tumble. We were visiting a friend's lodge in the woods for a gathering of folks I had known and loved in my growing-up years. Naturally, I wanted a group photo. Everyone lined up while I backed up to center the picture. *Why are they all yelling at me?* I wondered. "Stay still just another minute," I called out, oblivious to their waving arms and wild gestures. I never heard Steve yell, "Stop!" The next moment,

I was upside down, feet flying in the air, with my camera broken on the ground. I had backed right over a sawhorse, landing on the open blade of a saw. Miraculously, I wasn't hurt at all, but my pride was bruised.

How about the need for control? Most of us love to be in charge! We have our lives—and everyone else's—arranged clearly in our viewfinders. Why stop now? Control freaks, I'm convinced, have a harder time in life. Feeling that much responsibility for managing everything around us is exhausting! What a relief it is to hand the camera off to God. *Here, Lord, this is Your picture. You tell Your story any way You want to. Just line me up and tell me when to smile.*

Then there's fear: *God may not care what happens to me!* or *He might make me look foolish!* (It's clear to me now that I don't need God's help for that. I can do it effortlessly myself. Sometimes I think it's my spiritual gift.)

When I fear God might not be able to handle the seriousness of my problems or that He might not take care of me, I remember how Jesus' disciples felt when they were caught in a violent storm on the Sea of Galilee (see Mark 4:35-41). Fearing they would drown as the waves swamped their boat, somebody probably said, "Where's Jesus, anyway? Holy mackerel! There He is, sound asleep in the stern! Wake Him up, for heaven's sake!"

These guys had followed Jesus everywhere, even had given up their livelihoods. Now He was going to let them go down with the ship! Sure, they had spent plenty of time hearing Him preach and watching Him perform miracles. But when the crisis hit, even they were afraid Jesus might not, or could not, take care of them. They yelled, "Hey, teacher, don't you care if we drown?" (verse 38). How different is that from what you and I have said when we're afraid?

What did Jesus do? He calmly got up off His cushion, turned His face to the wind, and said, in effect, "Cut it out! Be quiet!" Silence. No more wind. Calm sea. Then Jesus turned and looked at His soaking-wet buddies and said, "Why are you so afraid? Do you still have no faith?" (verse 40). And they were terrified, as if they had seen a ghost. Actually, they had seen God, or had just begun to see Him. So have we.

The reason you and I get scared when we think we're going down is just the same as it was for the disciples: We have no idea who this Jesus is we're dealing with. Our idea of Him is way too small, too weak, and ill-informed. The truth is, He is all life, love, and truth in one Being. He is the One who came to lead us home in a very unexpected way—by overcoming far worse than a storm.

"What Are You Saying, Lord?"

God doesn't speak only through life's unexpected challenges; He speaks through unexpected opportunities, too—ones that He arranges. Serendipities help me hear Him say, "Look at what I have for you now!" But sometimes I wonder, *Can it really be God doing this?*

Several years ago, seemingly out of nowhere, I was asked to do an hour-long daily talk radio show, a frightening prospect for me. That would mean several hours each day working at the station producing the show (something I had never done before), doing research to prepare for interviews, and writing questions for my guests, not to mention learning how to do it all! But the knot in my stomach told me that none of those was the real problem. Working every day also meant I would not be available during those hours to meet the growing needs of my elderly mother or other family members. Someone else would have to take my place. Saying "no" to them even a few hours a day in order to say "yes" to God meant I had to be certain of His will. Was God aware of that little wrinkle? I had to be sure.

Wouldn't it be wonderful if God would just talk out loud to answer our questions? I'd love to hear, "Virelle, you can go this way if you want to, but there are big problems ahead. Why not take this other path instead?" How simple that would be! Fortunately, I've found that God does post road signs along my path that offer pretty clear direction.

I've learned to first look at the way my donkey is leaning. No doubt about it, God still directs us through circumstances in our lives. It could be an unexpected turn of events—either happy or sad—or some new dimension in our lives that requires wisdom or power beyond ourselves.

Remember when the wine ran out at a wedding Jesus was attending? (Having just had two of our children married in the past two years, running out of food or beverage is a parent-of-the-bride's nightmare.) When Mary told Jesus to do something, it was not optional. After all, Jesus was still her son. "My time has not yet come," He protested. It didn't work for Him, either. As only mothers know how to do, Mary simply pointed to the water jars nearby, directing the servants, "Do whatever He tells you," which is good advice for any of us. What happened next is history. Nobody forgot the wedding where Jesus performed His first miracle! (See John 2:1-11.) Jesus' wine was the best. It always is.

Sometimes I forget that Jesus is still in the miracle-working business. He's making fine wine out of my life and yours. No one can match His wine-making formula because each grape (that's us) is chosen by hand and grown in just the right way. Jesus makes wine out of our life stories to nourish a thirsty, dying world. Yet often my "whine" comes out first when I am squeezed by circumstances and poured out for others. I tend to do things backward. How much better it would be when the circumstances of my life take a sudden turn if I first asked, "Lord, what are You saying here?" and then did whatever He told me. Maybe it would change my crisis into a celebration!

Second, I listen for the whispers of God's Spirit. Isaiah 30:21 tells us, "Whether you turn to the right or to the left, your ears will hear a voice behind you, saying, 'This is the way; walk in it.'" Wouldn't it be nice if we recognized God's voice that easily? For years no one told me that the Holy Spirit often uses other people's voices to do His talking for Him.

As important as it was to hear God speak to me, negative voices inside my head almost drowned Him out. *You'll never be any good at this. You don't have the qualifications. You have no experience. No one will like your show.* So subtle are negative, critical, worrisome thoughts that they can almost sound humble, even quasi-spiritual. Sound familiar? I decided to tune out the static whine and listen to the voices I trusted: those of my husband, praying friends, my pastor, and some friends who had years of experience in Christian radio. They all said the same thing: "Do it! Do it! Do it!" I wondered, *Could that be God?*

Third, I go directly to the Guidebook. Funny thing about God: He always agrees with Himself. Every word of His— whether written in the Bible, whispered to our hearts, or lived out in our circumstances—will be in agreement. Gail MacDonald—author, speaker, and patient mentor of mine many years ago—explained to me one day that we're most likely to hear God speak to us personally when we are saturated in His Word, soaked through and through. Gail imprinted this on my life, teaching me to open my Bible each day with the expectation that God indeed has things to say to me. As I've savored His Word and even committed parts of it to memory, I've discovered that just when I need it, when a choice or a crisis comes, God drips sweet morsels of His Word into my conscious mind. The living Word speaks to me, feeding me like honey from a honeycomb!

Once during a health crisis with one of our children, I sat in the hospital waiting room, desperate for God to speak to me. Only one verse came to mind:

> *Why are you downcast, O my soul?*
> *Why so disturbed within me?*
> *Put your hope in God,*
> *for I will yet praise him,*
> *my Savior and my God.*
> (Psalm 42:11)

One verse, but it was all I needed.

One morning, as I prayed about the radio job, God's counsel seemed to drop right into my lap. I read in Isaiah:

> How beautiful on the mountains
>> are the feet of those who bring good news,
> who proclaim peace,
>> who bring good tidings,
>> who proclaim salvation,
> who say to Zion,
>> "Your God reigns!"
> (Isaiah 52:7)

That was it! I could picture radio waves beaming over the mountains bringing good news, peace, and salvation to listeners. I would invite guests who would build people up, tackle their most important life issues, even tickle their funny bones, and tell the true story of Christ's life in them. What good news that is! I would call the show "Real Life," because knowing Jesus is the only real life there is.

RELEASING OUR GRIP

Handing over the reins to God is often a daily affair, even if there are milestone moments that frame the official "handing off." In my framed memories is a scene much like the storm the disciples experienced. It blew in one summer at our wilderness camp in the Adirondack Mountains.

We bought the property on Union Falls Lake, just north of Whiteface Mountain, when our children were young. It fell into our laps, really—another serendipity. Our Robinson Crusoe-type camp is built into a steep hillside and is composed of two buildings on stilts: a bunkhouse and a kitchen cabin (oh, and a once-elegant outhouse). Our camp is approximately two miles down the seven-mile-long mountain lake on the side opposite where we put in our fourteen-foot aluminum boat, right near the waterfalls, and boating in over the lake is the only way to get there. On the remote side with us are bears, a few moose, eagles, osprey, and old logging trails. There is no road, no electricity, no running water, and, obviously, no phone. Did I mention no neighbors? Just us and nature's magical beauty—except when the weather changes and the surrounding mountains create a wind-tunnel effect, quickly whipping up treacherous whitecaps down the middle of the lake. Then nobody can leave the camp and nobody can boat in.

While Steve and I were spending a week at the lake with our newly married daughter and son-in-law, Lauren and Michael, the pair decided to leave a day ahead of us to head back home. That evening, Steve helped them pack up the boat with their mountain of gear, and I pushed them off the beach. As Steve gassed up the old seven-horsepower motor, he waved goodbye to me. "I'll be back in twenty minutes. I promise I'll hurry!" I had never been alone at the lake before, not even for a few minutes.

I waited until I could hear the boat round the point of the bay and head down the lake toward the campground where Lauren and Michael would disembark. As I turned to go up the stone steps to the kitchen cabin, a sudden rush of wind and rain slammed my back and pushed me forward. Darkness descended so quickly that I could barely see my way. I knew my husband and kids were in serious danger. So was I.

While rushing to get into the cabin, I grabbed a hammer off the window ledge to nail down the storm windows before all the light was gone. The lake was dark and roily; thunder boomed. *What if lightning hits our boat?* I considered with dread. *They're out in the middle of the lake by now! Oh, God, help them! Help me, too!*

Just as I nailed the last window down and secured the hooks that held it fast, a deafening jolt of thunder and lightning tore the sky. I fell back as if I'd been hit myself. I cried out to God, "Lord, what have You allowed? Don't You care if my family dies on the lake? Oh, God, help us!"

I cried long and hard in the dark at the kitchen table while lightning continued to flash every few seconds and rain pounded at the windows. When I finally stopped crying, I realized it was almost pitch dark. I found matches on the counter and attempted to light the propane lantern. It flooded and whooshed and died and then finally started. I reached for my Bible. Turning to the Psalms, I groped for meaning in my newly darkened world. What met me was hope in these words and many others like them:

> *In my alarm I said,*
> *"I am cut off from your sight!"*
> *Yet you heard my cry for mercy*

> *when I called to you for help.*
> *Love the* LORD, *all his saints!*
> *The* LORD *preserves the faithful,*
> *but the proud he pays back in full.*
> *Be strong and take heart,*
> *all you who hope in the* LORD.
> (Psalm 31:22-24)

I prayed in anguished surrender: "Father, I know You love me and You love my family. If they are dead, I know they are with You. If there's any part of me left after this, please keep it all. I give You the rest of my life."

About an hour later, the rain still pounded the lake, but the wind had died down and the lightning had ceased. I heard a faint, familiar sound coming from the lake. Closer now, it was clearly a boat motor. Was someone coming to get me, to tell me about my family? I opened the cabin door and strained to see through the darkness. A boat groaned toward our shore and stopped. A lone soaked figure stepped out and pulled the boat up on the beach, securing the rope to a tree.

"Steve! Is that you? Is that you?" I called out.

"Hi, honey, it's okay. We're all okay," he answered, slowly climbing the hill to meet me.

"Oh, thank God! Thank God!" Tears of relief and joy flooded my eyes.

Steve looked weak and exhausted. It was clear he was shivering, chilled to the bone. I lit the propane heater and made him a cup of hot tea while he changed from his drenched clothes into a sweat suit and dry socks and relayed what had happened.

"The lightning struck just as Lauren and Mike stepped onto the dock. Somehow, I wasn't hit. I spent the next few hours in the campground lean-to, where someone brought me a dry shirt. Lauren and Mike ran to their car and drove to Lake Placid for the night. I'm sure they're okay. It was a miracle, really. I'm amazed we weren't killed."

So was I. Amazed, thankful—and changed.

Life isn't "safe." Dangers no one can anticipate may await. Trusting God to lead us on this adventure called life means, at times, asking Him to lead us on a path wide enough for only One. When we hand God the reins, He leads us on our narrow, sometimes treacherous and frightening, paths. We ride our donkey hanging on for dear life, having no idea how it will all turn out. I have learned, from riding around enough blind curves, that it's enough to know that the One who calms our storms and whispers His promises in the dark is also the One guiding our donkey down the steep canyon. At least we know where He's headed—He's headed home.

Face to Face

• Do you have a white-knuckle grip on the reins of your life? What frightens you most about letting go? Oswald Chambers has helped me many times to hand my "what-ifs" to God. Today, for example, in my own dark time, I find these words:

At times God puts us through the discipline of darkness to teach us to heed Him. Songbirds are taught to sing in the dark, and we are put into the shadow of God's hand until we learn to hear Him. "What I tell you in darkness"— watch where God puts you into darkness, and when you are there keep your mouth shut. Are you in the dark just now in your circumstances or in your life with God? Then remain quiet. If you open your mouth in the dark, you will talk in the wrong mood: darkness is the time to listen.[1]

If you are in a dark time now, listen carefully for what God has to say to you. Don't lose it. Write it down and let Him speak to you again and again, as Psalm 94:18-19 speaks to me today:

When I said, "My foot is slipping,"
  your love, O LORD, supported me.
When anxiety was great within me,
  your consolation brought joy to my soul.

Do you feel His love supporting you today? Thank Him for the outcome toward which He is leading you. God is good—all the time.

- Do you have a "listening place" where you meet God sometime every day with an "open-eared" heart? Is there any way you might be hardening your heart, not willing to hear God's voice (or obey Him if you did)? We all need to tune out the daily static—the noisy demands of our busy lives and of others, even our own self-centered or critical voice. Getting quiet enough to listen takes unhurried time, more than five minutes, to tune in God's voice and listen. Right now, plan a couple of hours to get alone with God in the near future.

- Have you experienced anything like my storm at the lake? What was your crisis? How did it change you? Did God answer your cries for help in a surprising way?

- Possibly the answer was not what you wanted. How has that affected your view of God? Is there a verse in Scripture that has helped you trust God in a crisis?

- Picture your life twenty, thirty, or forty years from now. What will your legacy be like if you hand God the reins or if you do not? Write a prayer of response to God.

Truth for the Surefooted Journey

I know, O Lord, that a man's life is not his own; it is not for man to direct his steps. (Jeremiah 10:23)

The eternal God is your refuge, and underneath are the everlasting arms. (Deuteronomy 33:27)

CHAPTER FOUR

Saddle Sores

IT'S A GOOD thing that we don't know which donkey is going to show up next. Some mornings I might not have gotten out of bed had I known the discomfort the next burro would bring.

I'm a fan of *The Far Side* comic strip. One of my favorite cartoons features a dog riding in the backseat of the family car. Ears flying in the wind, he leans smugly out the car window and calls to his dog buddy Biff, who is confined in his fenced-in yard. "Ha, ha, ha, Biff!" he jeers. "Guess what? After we go to the drugstore and the post office, I'm going to the vet's to get tutored!"

How like that dog we are! We think we know where our lives are headed, and the plan looks good, even inviting. But the reality seldom matches the plan, and soon we find ourselves at the vet's, too. Definitely not our idea. You've been there, haven't you? It helps to hold tightly to a sense of humor.

As I write this, I've just spent three weeks in a most uncomfortable saddle, recovering from a severe back problem that had left me unable to walk, turn over, get dressed, or even pour a cup of coffee. Thankfully, rest, prayer, painkillers, and a fabulous caregiving husband have brought relief. The trouble is, there's a big difference between a short, inconvenient detour such as an injured back and a long journey on a donkey you never, ever wanted to ride.

Painful Realities

Evelyn sat in my family room recently and told a story about a road she and her husband, Mark, took but never would have chosen. They look like a family whose dreams have finally come true. These two bright, creative adults found each other in a Christian singles group. Their marriage led to expanded ministry, a beautiful new house, three lively little sons, and even a BMW as the family car. The American dream, it would seem, until their middle child, Tyler, began to display unusually stormy behavior, withdrawal from affection, and the inability to talk. Their dream turned into dreaded reality after a developmental pediatrician and a team of therapists evaluated Tyler when he was two and a half. The diagnosis came back as pervasive developmental disorder, a form of autism.

Tears came quickly as Evelyn chronicled their struggle over a year later. "I prayed. I cried, mostly in the shower—the only time my brain could unravel long enough to despair. I lost five pounds overnight."

Week by week, the reality of Tyler's condition began to unfold as Evelyn and Mark watched their son in the church nursery. "Tyler would circle the nursery, his sippy cup gripped tightly in the crutch of his arm, walking on his toes, tensing and screaming if any adult or child other than me approached him.

He had little interest in family or others, and I cringed at the thought of him growing up unable to make friends."

Had God forgotten to be kind? Did His goodness and mercy fail? Why this heartbreaking condition that blocked all response, vocal or otherwise, to the love they showed their son? Could anything hurt two highly verbal, emotive parents more? But they knew one reality had not changed: God loved them, and they opted to trust Him.

The turning point for Evelyn came at church while she watched a video of the New Testament story of Jesus healing the crippled and the mute. Evelyn sat up straight. Tyler was functionally mute! Having been raised in Africa in a missionary family, she had heard the story many times. How had that word, *mute,* slipped by her? For the first time, she understood how that mother must have felt when her son came home talking after Jesus healed him.

"I suddenly realized," Evelyn said, her voice rising with joy, "that praying for healing had nothing to do with greediness. Christ loved Tyler!" So she asked Him to heal Tyler, too, joining with our pastor and others who rested warm hands on her squirmy son.

Nothing happened right away. Then Tyler had the opportunity to attend a special school for autistic children. Reports of his progress trickled back to her while she and Mark found encouragement meeting other parents who also stared autism in the face. Gradually, a change began to take place in her son. One day he waved to his bus driver and said, "Bye." That was it—just "Bye." One by one, more words were added, more eye contact, more hugs. Evelyn wept for joy when she told me that Tyler is now, one year later, talking in sentences and has a downright sunny personality. Evelyn has a song of praise to sing for others who need encouragement, too.

But what about those whose stories don't have such happy endings, at least not ones we can see? Frankly, those are the stories I least like to tell. I'm definitely a "happy ending" type of person. Then I met a woman without one yet, whose whole persona lingers in my mind.

Nancy had offered to house two faculty members for the Christian writers' conference. A quiet, attractive woman with gentle blue eyes and long graying hair, she greeted Linda and me at the door when we arrived late one night. "Welcome," she said. "You can take your things upstairs to the room on the right. Then come down to the kitchen and have a snack." As we went upstairs, I looked down at the living room below. It was simple, artistic, and lovely. There was something special about this home.

A few minutes later, the three of us sat around the table in Nancy's kitchen. Family artwork decorated the walls, a teapot whistled softly on the stove, and a bowl of apples and bananas graced the middle of the table. There was no husband mentioned, and I wondered if Nancy lived alone. She made us a hot mug of herbal tea, and we each ate a piece of fruit while we talked. I found Nancy a remarkably beautiful person, soft-spoken, and an interested listener. We learned she had begun writing children's Sunday school curricula a few years earlier. Suddenly, she said, "Would you like to meet my husband?"

"Of course," we both mumbled, shocked at her mention of a husband at this point.

"Follow me," she said. "Ralph can hear you, but he can't speak." It was our only preparation as she led us through the mudroom to a beautiful large addition in the back of the house, a hospital room decorated in soft pastels and more artwork by her children. There lay her husband in a corner hospital bed with the sides drawn up. He was a handsome gray-haired man in his mid to late fifties, eyes closed, arms and legs folded up like a tired child.

"Ralph, these are our guests," she said, patting his shoulder. Ralph never responded. Linda shot me a painful glance, as though she wanted me to speak first.

I rested my hand on his shoulder and said, "Ralph, thank you for letting us stay in your home. It's good to meet you." Linda added a few kind words, and we turned to leave as Nancy kissed her husband good night.

Back at the kitchen table, Linda and I sat speechless. "Nancy, what happened?" I asked.

The story Nancy shared has never left me. She was a stay-at-home mom married to a handsome young engineer with a promising career. They had two little girls, ages four and six, when Ralph suffered a massive cerebral hemorrhage. It seemed impossible that he would live, but he did. Nancy decided to keep Ralph at home and care for him herself, even though it meant little sleep, no freedom or time for herself, and raising their two little girls alone. It was a long road she never had wanted to travel.

Nancy shared with me honestly about the many times she felt angry with God—even with Ralph—for their circumstances. "I'm like the son in the parable who said, 'No, I don't want to work in the field,' but did it anyway," she said, adding an afterthought. "In fact, I still grumble while doing it."

Who could handle the daily mountain of exhaustion, loneliness, and single parenting that she climbed while caring for an invalid husband, not to mention all her dying dreams for their future? No one I know. Somewhere along the way, she slumped helplessly in God's lap and gave up trying to deal with her life in her only-human strength.

"I spent ten years searching for answers to why God allows things like this to happen to people," Nancy continued. "Those 'why' questions still pop up in my mind whenever there is a new crisis. Each time, God shows me His love, care, and provision for us, often through the help and prayers of others." Gradually a transformation took place. Day by day, God gave her what she needed most: Himself, all of Him, stretching around her like a tight embrace. Nancy's inner beauty reflects that. The Source is evident.

To this day, Nancy is embedded in my heart as a woman who lives out the extremities of faith every day and has not quit. Christ's likeness rings as true as a tuning fork in her life. But she's no "too-good-to-be-true" Christian. When dealing with the often unfair realities of life, she hammers heaven with the same questions we all do. If I were Nancy I'd be asking, "When will this end? How much longer must I endure?" Perhaps you're asking God the same thing.

THREE QUESTIONS WITHOUT GOOD ANSWERS

When the rewards seem slim and the trials daunting, it gets harder and harder to live the Christian life. Like runners who "hit the wall," many quit. Others without faith seem to have it so much easier.

We all wrestle with the common questions suffering raises. I'm learning that God can handle our toughest questions just fine. We do not need to feel guilty when we storm the gates of heaven with pleas of anguish, even anger. God wants us to approach Him boldly and wholeheartedly. He wants to speak to us in our greatest times of need. Most of all, He wants to be as close to us during those times as the air we breathe.

"WHAT ABOUT *THEM*?"

Do you ever wonder why some Christians have so many problems? It seems unfair. Maybe you are one of them. Then there are others with seemingly none or very few. They have loving husbands, and you have none; they have a promising career, and you just got demoted or lost your job; they are the picture of vitality, and you are on your third round of antibiotics this year. The list goes on and so do our questions.

One of my favorite memories of my trip to Israel last summer is of dipping my toes in the water along the pebbled beach in Galilee where Jesus had appeared to His disciples early one morning following His resurrection. He called out to His friends in the boat, telling them to lower their nets yet again after a long, hard night of fruitless fishing. When they hauled in a mother lode of 153 big fish, they knew the man had to be Jesus. Best of all, He had a fire going and breakfast ready (see John 21:9-12).

It seems the occasion was chiefly for Peter's benefit, the disciple who had denied Jesus three times. It was enough to humble and restore Peter, making him a lifelong celebrant of God's mercy and grace. But there was more. In the same breath as "Feed my sheep," Jesus told Peter how he would die: "I tell you the truth, when you were younger you dressed yourself and went where you wanted; but when you are old you will stretch out your hands, and someone else will dress you and lead you where you do not want to go" (John 21:18). In other words, Peter would face crucifixion, too.

This did not sit well with Peter. Turning and pointing to John, he complained, "Lord, what about him?" (John 21:21).

In a most unsatisfying answer, Jesus said to Peter, "If I want him to remain alive until I return, what is that to you? You must follow me" (John 21:22). Not much help to Peter, was it?

The fact is, God deals with each of us individually. There is no "fair and square" system for divvying out suffering or blessings. Many Christians today face martyrdom, yet others grow old and die with their children and grandchildren around them. Why is that? God offers no explanation other than, "What is that to you? You must follow me. There is kingdom work to be done."

Wait a minute! you might be thinking. *This sounds like a not-very-nice side of Jesus! Couldn't He have said something a little more uplifting to Peter at a time like that? Wasn't Peter already feeling bad enough?* I've thought that myself. I mean, maybe He could have offered Peter a little heavenly carrot, something like, "Peter, you will have a huge reward in heaven. Just don't flinch when you find out what you have to do to get it, okay?" At least that would have helped me had I been in Peter's sandals.

Sometimes I'd like Jesus to give me more satisfying answers, too. I'm learning that when He doesn't, He gives me something much better. As He did for Nancy, He gives me Himself and all the power of heaven. And He never leaves. When I feel myself "hitting the wall," which is more often than I'd like, and simply cry, "Help me, Lord!" in some way, He always does.

"WHAT ABOUT *ME*?"

When Joyce Meyer spoke at a conference recently, she told the story of waking up in bed one Saturday morning mentally rehearsing a "honey-do" list for her husband. Then she realized he had already settled in to watch a ball game on TV.

Before her feet hit the floor, Joyce was seething at him, when suddenly the Holy Spirit spoke to her: "Joyce, you're just like a little robot that marches around saying, 'What about me? What about me? What about me?'" I joined thousands of women rocking with laughter as Joyce marched robot-style around the stage, parroting, "What about me? What about me? What about me?" It's funny in retrospect, but at the time, Joyce knew that God wanted her to change—immediately!

My struggle with discontent has run along the same line for years, resurfacing from one year to the next in many different guises. I'm usually blind to it for a long time. Whether it's grumbling over a too-small kitchen or not enough storage space or midlife weight that won't budge or my husband's favorite old car he won't replace, discontent is a mist that clouds my enjoyment of life too often. One thing's for certain: *That* donkey will bray on my doorstep again (and again).

What does Jesus want us to do with our own petulant version of "What about me?" I'm learning to do two things. First, pray no more vague prayers. I now pray absolutely honestly about the things that bother me, telling God the truth about how I really feel. Second, I'm practicing being thankful long before His answers come.

That's the real challenge: thanking Him ahead of time, before even a little rainbow of promise appears. Funny thing about the donkeys God allows: Sometimes they take us to the edge of the precipice, with no guardrail, no visible safety net below. There, on the edge, God asks us to trust Him and be thankful. That's tough!

Early in our marriage, my donkey was an unbelieving husband. I thought I was riding pretty well as a brand-new believer. I faithfully attended church with my three-year-old daughter. I joined a Scripture-memory class, taught children's vacation Bible school, and prayed up a storm. The problem was on the home front. I was wretched to my donkey husband, attributing every problem in the universe to his stubborn heart.

I got stopped in my self-righteous tracks one Sunday when I heard God's voice come right out of my donkey's mouth. Having arrived home from church with Lauren, I found Steve still unshaven and in his bathrobe, still plunked in front of the TV watching a ball game. He looked the same as he had when

I'd left him, only now he was hungry.

"What's for lunch?" he asked flatly.

I didn't even answer but marched to the kitchen to slap together a few hamburgers and some green beans. I slammed the plates and forks onto the table. *Lord, why do I have to put up with this?* I railed. *Why hasn't he changed? Look at him! Is he ever going to become the man I want him—You want him—to be?*

When the three of us were seated at the table, Lauren offered a simple prayer of thanks for the drab food. Steve had the nerve to ask, "How was church?"

"It was wonderful," I replied coldly. "You would have known that if you'd been there."

"I don't think I belong with those people. I'm not like them," he answered quietly, adding almost kindly the words that froze me in my tracks. "You know, if I were you, I'd feel guilty."

"Guilty? Me, guilty?!" I exploded, slamming my hand on the table. (Lauren quickly exited to the living room to watch cartoons.) "How can you say that? You're the one who doesn't believe! You're the one who stays home! You're the problem, not me!"

"That's true," he replied softly. "I am a pagan, and I'm behaving exactly the way a pagan is supposed to behave. But you're the Christian, and you're not loving."

I was stunned, speechless. Quickly, I cleared the table, threw the dishes in the sink, ran up to our bedroom, and locked the door. On my knees, I cried out to God, "Lord, You know that's not true! Look at everything I've done to follow You, to pray, to commit myself to You. Now this. It's not fair! You know he isn't right, don't You?"

The silence from heaven was deafening. With a sick thud in my spirit, suddenly I knew that God agreed with Steve. I was an unloving wife. In fact, I was a miserably critical woman, always comparing him with other women's husbands who I thought were strong Christians, loved their wives more, went to church, and lived the way they were "supposed" to. Now what was I supposed to do?

Softly, God's voice spoke to my heart: "Virelle, what is it you really want?"

Wiping my tears on the bedspread, I answered simply, "I just want him to believe in You, Lord. That's all."

"Can you thank Me now for it, even if he doesn't believe for thirty years or you never get to see it?"

"Oh, Lord, that's not what I want!" But that's what God offered. Would I take it or not? "Okay, Lord. I'll try to learn how to let that be enough for me." I cried some more.

"Then love him now," God whispered with great kindness, "as if he were already the man you want him to be, the man I want him to be. And thank Me for the answer even if you don't get to see it. It will come in My time."

That was it—a gut-level exchange in ten minutes or less. God went right for my jugular vein, my will. He left me limp and honestly sorry for being a rotten Christian at home.

"This is my commandment," Jesus says (John 15:12, ESV), "that you love one another as I have loved you." I had a barely trickling stream of love flowing in my life when what I really needed was an ocean. I had to learn the hard way that God's love has nothing to do with sentiment or warm fuzzies. In fact, love is often more like work. Love costs time given when it's very inconvenient. It trains us to be silent, or at least kind, when misunderstood and to be patient with those who are weaker than we are in body, faith, or mind. It's impossible love made possible when God fills us with Himself.

When I first confessed to Steve that what he said was true, he thought it was just another ploy to get him to go to church. Learning to love again took work. I had long stopped considering how to be a loving wife to my husband. I started very small — by bringing him coffee while he was shaving. Then I worked on my tone of voice and the attitude that dictated it. That was much harder, and I found myself coming back into the room often to say I was sorry. Most important, God reminded me regularly to be thankful that He was at work in my donkey's life and He didn't need my help — or my words.

I don't know who changed first, but over the months that followed, my formerly donkey husband turned into the object of my deep affection once again. Our marriage, though unequal in faith, became happy again. I stopped asking Steve to go to church, stopped witnessing to him or setting him up. Instead, a sweet older man, a Christian who'd ridden a few donkeys himself, invited Steve fishing, and God, without words, hooked Steve's heart with His perfect love.

Decades have passed since God taught me a whole lot I needed to know about how He works. Now when I find myself asking "What about me?" I'm much more likely to remember an idea I believe God gave me about prayer several years ago. A light went on in my head one day: Why not write down all my most impossible prayers and give them to God, especially the ones that look too hard even for Him? I wrote out ten "impossible" prayers on a 3 x 5 card and put it in my Bible. Every few days, I'd bring out my list and pray through it: "Lord, whatever You can do with this would be great! We need a miracle!"

Then I began to thank God just for listening to me, for taking on my concerns as His own. I thanked Him for His answers whether they matched my plans or not. And one by one, He did give me His answers. Sometimes I loved them; sometimes I didn't. It's been eight years since I began that experiment in prayer. Every year, I refine my list, recording answers as they come in. I'm still waiting for quite a few, but more than half, perhaps closer to three-quarters, of my "impossible" prayers have been answered. Most important, my trust in God, expressed in a thankful heart, has ballooned. I'm far more content, even loving, than I used to be—even though I still have a long way to go.

"WHY DOES IT HAVE TO HURT SO MUCH?"

This could be the most Christlike question of all. Jesus cried out from the cross, "My God, my God, why have you forsaken me?" (Matthew 27:46). If Jesus felt abandoned, will we not feel the same when God allows painful trials? We deceive others and ourselves when we don't admit grief, pain, discouragement, and despair.

Consider Ralph. He can't respond aloud, but Ralph hears and understands everything. On his Eyegaze computer system, Ralph is able to communicate by using the tiny muscles in his right eyeball. Often, when his attendant rolls him up to the computer in a wheelchair, he types, "ILOVENANCYVERYMUCH," all in caps with no spaces in between. Then he "hits" the visual "speak" button, and the computer's voice synthesizer says it out loud. "Some days," Nancy told me, "it's enough to get me through the day."

But on another occasion, Ralph typed out, "GODISVERY-HARDONME." Nancy responded by reading Scripture to him. Especially helpful was reading aloud Joni Eareckson Tada's book coauthored with Steve Estes *When God Weeps.*

"Ralph has shown great faith and courage," Nancy told me. "One day he gave me a small hand squeeze, meaning 'yes,' when I read Joni's statement, 'Despite the pain, I would rather be in this chair knowing Him than on my feet without Him.' If I were in his situation, could I say the same thing? It made me respect Ralph even more."

Why does God let us hurt? Why did He let His own Son hurt? I don't know. I wish I did, but I can tell you His love and His deep hunger for us to know Him better is behind it all. Intimacy grows deep and sweet when we come to Him for comfort and help.

My father-in-law showed me this sweetness in the "daddy-hood" of God one day. We had been talking over an extended breakfast about our children, their needs as teenagers, the struggles each one had. I was more fragile than I realized over my son Bob's rebellion. He had rocked our family boat a lot that year, pushing us all to the breaking point many times, but he was still my son. When my father-in-law made the simplest comment about his difficult behavior, my heart rose fiercely in his defense. I exploded in anger and ran upstairs in tears.

Steve and his folks sat at the breakfast table in stunned silence. This had never happened before and never has since. I love my in-laws deeply. They are nearly perfect in my mind. Where did this outburst come from? In a few minutes, I came back downstairs to apologize to everyone and met my father-in-law already coming up to meet me, arms extended to me. "I'm so sorry," he said. "I'm so sorry to have hurt you." He folded me in a tight embrace, and I cried again. I think he cried, too.

That's what God is like. Even when we're at our worst, railing at Him in tears over the things He's allowed, He loves us more than we could ever deserve. His daddy-heart wraps us in a tight embrace.

THE BLESSINGS OF OBEDIENCE

So what can we do to make God glow with pleasure over us? Lead a perfect life? Certainly not. Give Him every ounce of energy, every buck in the bank, every "ought-to" on our list? Don't think so. What then?

Not much is said today about the blessings of obeying God. We tend to seek a freedom not rooted in the truth of Scripture— the freedom to do as we please, to welcome the longings and directives of the most wounded and needy parts of ourselves, the kind of freedom that never sets us free from the bondage to self. The soaring freedom we seek is actually found in an unlikely place: obedience. It is a listening place that will teach us ways to relate to God and others that release us from the enslavement of fear and self-will. The following are just some of the things we learn through hearing and obeying God's voice.

WE LEARN TO WAIT ON GOD.

Waiting again. It's the no-fun part of being a Christian. I'm learning now that waiting has as much to do with the posture of our hearts as it does with the passage of time. Sometimes the time we wait is insignificant. It's the heart bowed to honor Him, quieted enough to listen, expectant of His goodness and mercy, that God is after. It's a heart that believes God will give everything we need just because He loves us. Extreme faith opens its mouth wide and knows God will fill it.

What would extreme obedience look like in your life? Would it mean moving someplace that doesn't excite you? Caring for someone who is needy? Giving something costly like time, talent, prayer, or forgiving grace? Would it mean letting God choose your future for you? In Nancy's life, it meant saying simply, "Yes, I will"—a no-frills prayer strictly for grown-ups.

WE LEARN TO GIVE UP OUR OWN WAY.

As Nancy did, we come to realize we have no control at all and really never did:

> I realized anew just this spring that I am powerless to direct the course of events. My mother was dying and we had less attendant care for Ralph than we've had in eleven years. Then the same day I learned my

mother's illness was terminal, I received a wedding invitation from my niece in Egypt with plane tickets included! I didn't see how I could go. I felt so stressed and torn that I began having physical problems: sleeplessness, rapid heart rate, weight loss, anxious-ness over little things. I said I was trusting God to work it all out but didn't really believe it in my heart. Then my mother died on a Sunday, and the funeral was that next Friday. People offered to care for Ralph, and I left for Cairo the Monday after the funeral. God took care of everything.

Recognizing we aren't in control has its benefits. We can finally relax. The fight is over. The responsibility for leading this donkey is now God's—and His alone. What a relief!

WE LEARN SENSITIVITY TO OTHERS' PAIN.

Telling the story of the traveler who was beaten, robbed, and left for dead, Jesus describes the religious types who walked a wide circle around the victim. But not the Samaritan. Already an out-cast, he knew how to care for another. Bandaging him, pouring oil and wine on his wounds to cleanse them, "he put the man on his own donkey [how wonderful!], took him to an inn and took care of him" (Luke 10:34). His mercy spoke volumes to Jesus' listeners. "Go," He said, "and do likewise" (verse 37). Wounds often qualify us to serve others.

Even though Nancy admits being less tolerant now of people's small complaints, she's sought out by caregivers and divorced friends who need help handling loneliness. "Sometimes I just listen," she said. "I try to steer them toward deeper intimacy with Jesus. That is what has made all the difference for me."

WE LEARN TO FOCUS ON ETERNITY.

"Truly, truly," Jesus says to you and me, "whoever [that's us] hears my word and believes him who sent me has eternal life. He does not come into judgment, but has passed from death to life" (John 5:24, ESV). Belief sounds easy until it means staking your life on it. God knew it would be hard; that's why He underscores His promise twice: "Truly, *truly. . . .*" Jesus wants us to know beyond a doubt that He can be trusted to lead us all the way Home. Eternal life with Him, which begins the moment we invite Christ into our lives, is our sure destiny. Once we have that settled, the challenges we face on earth, even when they feel devastating, are actually small in comparison.

A year and a half ago, my daughter's lifetime best friend, Birgitta—whom we loved like a daughter—died two days before her thirty-fourth birthday while giving birth to her fourth baby. It was a stunning blow to her family, to Lauren, and to all of us. I keenly remember hugging Birgitta when she was a little girl. She hopped down our stairs many times in her robe and pajamas during sleepovers. We often still weep out loud when we think of Birgitta and how precious she was to all who knew and loved her. But Birgitta is alive with Jesus, and we know it. I can't tell you how much the truth of Jesus' promise in John 5:24 impacts me.

Birgitta's parents came to visit us recently. They had just returned from the one-year memorial of Birgitta's death. Seldom have I seen such grace and thankfulness in the midst of grief as Sonny and Irene radiate. Where does it come from? They had learned long before their deepest trial that God's promises could hold them through every circumstance. Believing that His Word is true, His love rock solid, they know their dear Birgitta is safely Home. They miss her always but know they will be with her again in heaven for all eternity. And God's love will carry them every step of the way there.

WE LEARN TO INTERCEDE — THE MOST UNSELFISH THING WE CAN DO.

Oswald Chambers describes prayer as the most unselfish, important thing we can do, and yet much of our prayer life he describes as "a continual grubbing on the inside to see whether we are what we ought to be, . . . a self-centered, morbid type of Christianity, not the robust, simple life of the child of God."[1]

Nancy discovered that God saves His surprises for the moment we need them most. "He does it all the time!" she said. "Sending me to Egypt — which turned out to be the trip of a lifetime — was just one example."

My problems have been small compared to Nancy and Ralph's, yet often I feel like a magnet for others in their lowest moments. Friends in need call on a regular basis for prayer, a listening ear, and a place to share their stories safely. I am glad to be that safe place. But it would crush me to just listen if I didn't know for a fact that God is listening, too. He hurts along with us and longs to dry our tears. In fact, He promises to dry our tears. For now, He lets us dry them for one another and kiss them away with our prayers.

WE LEARN TO LOVE, EVEN WHEN OUR OWN NEEDS ARE NOT BEING MET.

Have you ever been called to love another when nothing was coming back your way? Neither appreciation nor returned love nor even an understanding of your own need for rest and care? It is the ultimate test of loving, one we all fail on our own. But God never does. His love rallies when ours drops from exhaustion. His lifts us for another day or another moment, right when we have nothing left to give. It is His love bubbling up through our dry veins that 1 Corinthians 13:3-8 describes as eternal, unchanging, and never failing:

> *I am bankrupt without love.*
> *Love never gives up.*
> *Love cares more for others than for self.*
> *Love doesn't want what it doesn't have.*
> *Love doesn't strut,*
> *Doesn't have a swelled head,*
> *Doesn't force itself on others,*
> *Isn't always "me first,"*
> *Doesn't fly off the handle,*
> *Doesn't keep score of the sins of others,*
> *Doesn't revel when others grovel,*
> *Takes pleasure in the flowering of truth,*

Puts up with anything,
Trusts God always,
Always looks for the best,
Never looks back,
But keeps going to the end.
Love never dies.
(MSG)

Nancy discovered what God's highest calling is: simply loving in God's strength, in His name. Hands down, it is the hardest thing we will ever do. Only God can infuse us with that kind of love. It is over our heads — out of our reach — but it is utterly like Him. God will give each of us all we need from the deep well of the Holy Spirit within us when we ask Him in faith. He is not only the Giver but also the gift of Love incarnate.

I need to know that today. Often, on the back of whatever donkey I happen to be riding, the biggest saddle sore I experience is the shortage of my own love toward those who need it. Mine is short-lived and self-centered, weak and puny under the weight of someone else's staggering needs. I chafe, laboring to meet those needs in my own strength, then soon collapse, sore and defeated. When I finally look up, though, I come face-to-face with the God who longs to provide everything I need. "Child," I hear Him say, "I will never leave you or forsake you. You have only to ask for help. All I have is yours."

Face to Face

- Have you ever traveled a long way on a road you never would have chosen, as Evelyn or Nancy did? What was it like? Are you still on that road? How has the experience changed you?

- In her book *Under the Circumstances*, Judy Hampton talks about a long period of discouragement when her husband, Orvey, was unemployed. One day while she was praying, she had a total change of heart as she thought of the verses in 1 Peter 1:6-7: "In this you greatly rejoice, though now for a little while you may have had to suffer grief in all kinds of trials. These have come so that your faith—of greater worth than gold, which perishes even though refined by fire—may be proved genuine and may result in praise, glory and honor when Jesus Christ is revealed." Judy describes her change of heart:

> *Our situation hadn't changed, but my viewpoint*
> *had. I knew God had a plan. My husband was still*
> *unemployed. But that day, I began to mature. It was*
> *a big step. I made a decision to trust the Lord—no*
> *matter what. For the first time in months, I felt joy. I*
> *had confidence not in our circumstances changing*
> *but in an unchanging God.*[2]

It's a huge step to trust the Lord no matter what happens. It seems to be a turning point in many lives, such as Judy's or Nancy's. Are you ready to shift in the saddle on your own painful donkey ride? Start by giving the outcome to God. Practice trusting Him to have your very best interests in mind. He loves you more than words can express.

• Read all of 1 Corinthians 13 in both *The Message* and the Bible version you normally use. Ask God to pinpoint areas in which your love needs to resemble His more. Ask Him to give you a willing spirit to love like He does.

• Do you ever ask, "What about *them?*" when others get what they want and you don't? Everyone asks that at one time or another. It helps to tell God all about your feelings and ask Him to help you sort them out. Is what God has given you "enough"? Can you still praise Him if He chooses not to give you what you want?

• Can you identify with my struggle with discontent? Are there similar things you feel discontent with at times? Why is "feeling cheated" such a subtle sin? Where does it lead? Name other "self" sins that trip you up. List them in your journal and ask a praying friend to support you as you continue to grow into the person God wants you to be.

Truth for the Surefooted Journey

*For we do not preach ourselves, but Jesus Christ as
Lord, and ourselves as your servants for Jesus'
sake. For God, who said, "Let light shine out of
darkness," made his light shine in our hearts to give
us the light of the knowledge of the glory of God in
the face of Christ.*

*But we have this treasure in jars of clay to show
that this all-surpassing power is from God and not
from us. We are hard pressed on every side, but not
crushed; perplexed, but not in despair; persecuted,
but not abandoned; struck down, but not destroyed.
We always carry around in our body the death of
Jesus, so that the life of Jesus may also be revealed
in our body.* (2 Corinthians 4:5-10)

*In this you greatly rejoice, though now for a little while
you may have had to suffer grief in all kinds of trials.
These have come so that your faith—of greater worth
than gold, which perishes even though refined by
fire—may be proved genuine and may result in
praise, glory and honor when Jesus Christ is
revealed.* (1 Peter 1:6-7)

CHAPTER FIVE

"ARE WE THERE YET, GOD?"

DONKEYS ARE THINKERS. They don't like to be forced to do anything—especially *hurry*. It's not that they can't; they just need a good reason. Unlike humans, they are cautious creatures that take their time and step carefully. Some donkeys in our lives that God either sends or allows can linger a long time, too. Oh, the maddening leisure of God! Just when we want Him to fast-forward this part of our journey, things slow down to a near halt. Ask any caregiver, parent of a prodigal, or person in recovery. It feels like swimming against the current.

Are you there right now? Do you wonder if you missed a turn somewhere? Do you find yourself asking, "Why, God? Why are You taking so long to get me through this? Couldn't You please hurry up the answer to my prayers?"

Waiting is necessary at times, but it's truly the hardest discipline to learn. When I was young, my father's worst punishment was to make me sit still in his overstuffed chair and be quiet for an hour. Impossible! Ask me to do anything else—clean my room, sweep the garage, anything!—but sit still and be quiet. What could I possibly learn from that? A lot, it turns out, such as listening with an open heart.

I'm certain God has better plans than to make us miserable. He promises good plans, blessings and abundance, joy and peace. Then why the wait? Perhaps more than answering our prayers right this minute, more than resolving today's frustrations, God wants time with us — time to talk intimately, time to share our lives. He wants to tune our ears to His voice, awaken our spirit to His whispers, turn our eyes to meet His, and empower our hearts to love Him and others in ways we simply can't do without becoming more like Him. This kind of transforming intimacy takes time and association.

When our kids were growing up, they probably got tired of hearing me say, "Be careful who your friends are; you'll become just like them." But it's true of all of us, no matter what our age. Think of the people whose influence is embedded in your life, for good or for bad. Without realizing it, we become like those we spend time with, especially those we love and admire. We gesture like them, laugh like them, develop some of the same likes and dislikes, and absorb their values. I have many of the same tastes as my Aunt Ginny who wore red glasses ten years before the rest of the world thought it was cool.

Last night, my newly married son phoned while Steve was attending a Christian men's conference with our son-in-law Jim. Dave said, "Tell Dad I'm sorry I couldn't be there with him. Tell him how many times I ask myself consciously, 'What would Dad say now?' Especially when I get angry or stressed, I consider, 'What facial expression would Dad use?' He's so kind, Mom. So strong. Dad's an oak." I agree. Both of our sons, Dave and Bob, resemble their dad in many ways because of the years father and sons have spent together.

Spending time with Jesus is just the same. The longer we "hang around Him," in His Word and with His followers, the more we become like Him without even realizing it. "That's why we can be so sure," wrote the apostle Paul, "that every detail in our lives of love for God is worked into something good. God knew what he was doing from the very beginning. He decided from the outset to shape the lives of those who love him along the same lines as the life of his Son" (Romans 8:28-29, MSG). What sometimes seems like a slow-motion journey on a series of very deliberate donkeys is what shapes our lives according to God's plan—when we're not even looking.

Paul writes from his own experience. It may seem he sky-rocketed onto the scene after his blinding-light conversion on the road to Damascus, but the real story tells us of Paul's ride on a very deliberate donkey. After his dramatic experience meeting Jesus, he spent the next three years in Arabia and later in Damascus quietly communing with God. Then, after a brief two weeks spent with Peter and James in Jerusalem, Paul submerged for another fourteen years. Doing what? Spending time with God, praying, doing some preaching—but mostly listening and changing from the inside out. Only then was Paul ready to step into his calling to bring the good news of Christ's salvation to a world dying of spiritual hunger. Just like we do, Paul needed time and intimacy with Jesus to grow into the leader God needed. (You can read more about Paul's faith journey in Galatians 1:11–2:2 and throughout the book of Acts.)

TASTY FRUIT TAKES TIME

Mention a perfectly ripe avocado or a bunch of luscious seedless grapes and I want one. But believe me, once you've tasted a perfect Macintosh apple from New York state, you're hooked. Crunching into one takes me back to my childhood along Lake Ontario in New York, famous apple-growing country.

Every fruit that's a positive part of our memory makes us want more. Steve grew up with homemade strawberry and peach shortcake, pies, and applesauce (the kind that makes him drool for more). It's that way with spiritual fruit, too. Tasting it in others' lives makes us want it for ourselves.

God uses ordinary Christians, imperfect as we are, to whet others' appetites for His character and love. The best part is, we are seldom aware of it at the time. Ginny and Keith were the loving people who first drew me to Jesus, patiently answering my questions about God when I threw down the gauntlet. They were kind and gentle, hospitable and helpful. Others generously provided a car when ours died and showed grace when my husband rejected their early attempts to share Jesus with him. Their fruit tasted unreal to me, divine, like nothing I'd ever experienced.

Maybe fruit tastes best when it's a love gift to someone else. Soon I wanted it more than anything in the world. I devoured whole books of the Bible in one large gulp, snacked all day on Christian literature, and drank in sermons and tapes, thinking I could grow up overnight into a strong believer like my friends. I soon discovered it wasn't as easy as I'd hoped. There's more involved in maturing spiritually than simply taking in good food. Growing tasty spiritual fruit doesn't happen overnight.

Unlike me, God isn't the kind of parent who hurries His children or rushes them through each stage of growth. He knows that good fruit takes time and the proper conditions to ripen. The fresh language of *The Message* puts it this way:

> *But what happens when we live God's way? He brings gifts into our lives, much the same way that fruit appears in an orchard—things like affection for others, exuberance about life, serenity. We develop a willingness to stick with things, a sense of compassion in the heart, and a conviction that a basic holiness permeates things and people. We find ourselves involved in loyal commitments, not needing to force our way in life, able to marshal and direct our energies wisely.* (Galatians 5:22-23)

Recently, we visited our oldest daughter, Lauren, and her husband, Michael, at their mountaintop home in western New York. They invited us on an adventure.

"Hey, come down and see how the orchard's coming along!" Michael gestured toward a wide mowed path down the hillside next to their house. The old orchard had been left untended and overgrown for twenty years before they bought the land, sixty acres facing an unspoiled view of spectacular sunsets. Disappointed that the fruit the orchard yielded was small and inedible, Michael felt challenged to revitalize it. For six years he trimmed away deadwood and lopped off heavy, hard-to-reach branches, opening up the lower branches of the ancient trees to the sun. Year after year, he mowed around the five remaining fruit trees until they began to bear fruit again—tons of it, in fact.

As I admired the burgeoning crop of apples, cherries, and pears, I thought to myself, *You've grown a lot more fruit than what is on these trees, kids.* It's been a long road for them since Lauren was diagnosed at the age of twenty-three with a debilitating form of systemic lupus, an autoimmune disease that causes her joint pain and extreme fatigue. Two years into her marriage, she went from being a very energetic, "type A" personality with an unlimited range of activities to being bedridden and unable to work at all for several years. It was like watching a football player taking a hit in a slow-motion replay—falling, falling, falling more. We were powerless to stop our daughter's downward spiral.

Lauren's a realist. Soon after being diagnosed, she researched her illness and courageously faced the possibilities of organ failure, a common occurrence in lupus. I hated seeing books in her living room about lupus and early morbidity. Even though we had a family friend who had died in her forties from lupus, for several years I was in denial about such a possibility, believing Lauren's diagnosis had to be a mistake. Or even if it were true, God would certainly heal her, wouldn't He? But so far, He hasn't.

Nobody found the reality easy. Michael often cried quietly to himself at night and spent long hours agonizing with God while hiking in the woods. Having come from large families, both

Lauren and Michael ached over the fact that having children one day was probably out of the question. Far worse was the prospect of increased disability and a lifestyle so different from the picture they had dreamed of since their college romance at Cornell.

Years went by, and with time, adjustment and acceptance gradually seeped into all of us. Lauren turned to God in His Word, seeking a face-to-face encounter in daily study and Scripture memorization. She cried out to Him for answers, for healing, for help.

Many times, God cared for Lauren and Michael by sending good gifts through close friends who prayed and brought meals, prayed and did laundry or cleaned their house, prayed and listened, prayed and invited Michael to go fishing or duck hunting. But the most extravagant gifts, by far, arrived several years later as God's grace walked them safely through two high-risk pregnancies. The birth of their son, Thane, was followed two years later by that of their daughter, Jillian.

In the dozen or so years since her diagnosis, Lauren's health has been a daily challenge. Her organs remain fine, her spirit tested but strong, but her body is often tired and in pain. As an environmental consultant, Michael maintains an office at home and is a daddy-on-call most of the time. As a couple, they have learned volumes about loving when it's lonely and difficult, balancing life between rest and work, family and ministry. But learning all this happened in slow motion—very slow motion.

Chronic illness is a donkey Lauren and Michael never wanted to see waiting at their door, but they are mastering the quieted ride day by day, encouraging other couples — through writing and teaching — in their marriage and family life. Fruit-bearing people have learned to let God do the pruning in their lives and to run to Him for the Living Water that keeps them alive, especially in times of prolonged stress and drought. I have had to learn that the hard way myself.

RUNNING DRY

Several times in my life, my inner "well" ran dry. Pumping out daily, refilled too seldom, I gave and gave out of my dwindling supply until there wasn't anything left to give. We had four teenagers or almost-teens with way too many activities, and I was the only driver, cook, and laundress. Every day was a marathon event on top of yesterday's race. One night I sat on the edge of the bed and began to cry.

"What's wrong?" Steve asked, alarmed. "Are you okay?"

"I think so," I sniffed.

"Then why are you crying?" he asked again, clearly mysti-fied. Men, even the best of them, just don't think like women!

"I guess I'm so tired. I need a rest and I don't know how to get one." Steve stayed home the next day to help me chauffeur kids, and he bought pizza for everyone. We prayed for a rest period to come.

It did. Another donkey arrived right on schedule. Hardly a month later, on a sightseeing trip with family and friends who were visiting, I fell flat on my face on a curb and slipped two disks in my back. I spent the next year in neck traction, wearing a cervical collar off and on to heal my neck and lower back. Twice every day for an hour at a time I sat captive behind our closed bedroom door with my head slung in a harness connected to a heavy bag of water. It was a little like being stretched on a rack, I presume, and did little or no good for my neck. What did heal, however, was my tired spirit.

Lest you think God was unkind in sending this slow-motion donkey, let me be quick to point out that this burro was the best blessing in my life. I finally learned how to rest. Not only did my kids and husband take over running the house for a year, which was a very good thing, but I spent two hours every day with my nose in my Bible. Three months into this process, my mind at last became quiet enough to hear God speak, and this is what He said:

> *"Come to me, all you who are weary and burdened [that would be me], and I will give you rest [musical words to this exhausted woman]. Take my yoke upon you [oh no, not more work!] and learn from me, for I am gentle and humble in heart [promise me You'll be gentle], and you will find rest for your souls [rest! yes, rest!]. For my yoke is easy and my burden is light."* (Matthew 11:28-30)

Hmmm. Just a minute, Lord. Your yoke is easy and light? Mine has not felt that way for a long time. Whose heavy burdens have I been lugging around? My own? Someone else's? Oh, Lord, I've been taking on more than You ever wanted me to. Forgive me. And please remind me in the future to ask You for supernatural strength and wisdom to carry whatever You give me. What's that? You'll carry the heavy end for me? Oh, thank You, Lord! Thank You!

That is just one of the soul-nourishing messages God communicated to this tired woman in traction. I grew to love the hours I spent reading my Bible in that neck contraption. My donkey became a treasured friend because it carried me into God's presence, where I heard Him speak words of love, affirmation, instruction, and encouragement. He poured Himself into my well each day until I was full again. And I learned how to stay full, drinking all I could each day.

There were few "normal" activities I could do while my back recovered. I could still cook and drive, but not much else. One day a notice appeared in the town library that stated the New York State Writers' Institute was hosting a free six-week evening class for new writers. I had always loved writing, had studied it in college, but had published only one article in a church newspaper. I mentioned the course to Steve that night.

"You've got to do it! We'll go together this week," he said enthusiastically. "We" went once. Steve was traveling a lot for his job, but I went every week. I wrote about the women who had most influenced my life. Then I read my pieces to Steve while he was shaving in the morning. One night in class, the writing instructor read my work to the group. She liked it and encouraged me to write a book, although that never was my intention.

"I'll put these little stories into a collection for our girls one day," I told Steve's foam-covered face the next morning.

"I think you should write a book," he replied. "Even if it takes two years. You can do it, I know you can." Steve, always so encouraging, had a far bigger dream than I did.

The book did take two years to write, and it never got published. But, in time (a very long time) another one did. Then there was another long wait while a second was conceived and birthed, and then another, and the process continues, in spite of many setbacks and discouragements: lots of waiting punctuated with moments of exhilaration and joy, followed by hours and hours of work that often feels more like worship.

It was a good donkey indeed that showed up at my door. It came at God's bidding in answer to my prayer for rest. This little fellow brought more than a new pastime; he brought a new call from God on my life, along with a message from God that I badly needed.

I now know that I need to tend to the well every day. Refills are free, but they are not optional. Running dry makes a lot of people suffer, especially me. When others around me, usually Steve or a close friend, see red lights flashing, "Warning! Virelle's nearing empty!" they are kind enough to ask, "Have you taken any time to renew yourself lately? Are you resting, having fun, just laughing a little?" Laughter is a very spiritual thing, you know. It's a built-in means of healing our minds and refreshing our tired souls.

I appreciate the thoughtful questions: "What are you doing to nourish yourself? Are you spending time with the Lord?" Those questions mean I'm loved, not judged. It's good to give someone else permission to ask you how you're doing. Do you have someone in your life who keeps you in check? If you do, you are both wise and rich.

Keeping the well filled enables us to become ripe for God's surprises, His next assignment or adventure, His next challenge. It may be the call in the middle of the night from a hurting friend, the opportunity to lead someone to Christ, or the chance to pour out a little of the grace we've been given. Will we be ready?

SINGING IN THE SADDLE

On any trip, one way to make the time pass faster is to sing in the car, on the bus, or in this case, in the saddle. How well I remember singing at the top of my lungs with all the other kids on bus rides to summer camp.

I've learned since then that my voice is, well, more like filler. It's passable, but I try not to be overheard too much. I've always envied singers. Listening to others with gifts of song leaves me mesmerized. *Lord, couldn't You have given me a good singing voice like theirs?*

What He gave me was the gift of gab (sometimes too much!). The only trouble I ever got into in school was for talking or giggling. Even as an adult, I was once asked to leave the church photo shoot for trying to make people laugh in their pictures. I think the photographer was just grumpy that day. (Incidentally, the pastor's wife was thrown out with me.) Steve and I were asked to be greeters at church only once in eighteen years. We had so much fun talking to people in the narthex that it disturbed those in the sanctuary. "Never again let the Kidders do that," someone must have ruled. At times, talking seemed more like a plague than a gift—that is, until one day, while walking up to the podium to make a simple announcement at church, I heard God whisper, "This is your song, Virelle. Sing it for Me."

Talking? Talking is my song, Lord? Why, yes—yes, it is! Thank You! Now I had one, too. Not a song like beautiful singers or pianists or other musical artists have. But I have my voice, the thing that so often ushered me to the doghouse. Now God lets me use it for Him. Every chance He gives me, I climb up on an imaginary altar and sing for Jesus.

Has God given you a talent that brings you joy every time you use it for Him? It may be serving others, management, strategic planning, hospitality, or athletics. Whatever it is, "singing it back to Him" brings God joy and makes your daily journey seem shorter and sweeter.

You may be reading this feeling seriously stalled en route. Is your donkey too deliberate, making such slow progress you feel like you'll never "get there"? I don't want to sound trite, but I encourage you to try something simple that I've found works: Just say "thank You" to God for where you are today, even if it's not where you want to be. Thank Him for His presence, even if you can't feel it, and invite Him to lead you all over again. If your well has run dry, take all the time you need to rest, asking God to fill you up with Himself. He will. Watch for His answers; they will come.

Growing up takes time. Preparation for ministry takes time, even if it's the least observed and least public kind of ministry.

That makes no difference. God sees and is pleased when we simply and humbly offer ourselves and our abilities to Him with a thankful heart. Then all the waiting, all the pruning, all the time spent listening to His voice on the journey is worth it.

∩ ∩

Face to Face

- Are you in a slow period right now? Perhaps you feel confused, even stalled, in your walk with God. Have you ever been there before? If so, what did you learn at that time? In what ways did it change you?

- What might God be developing in you now through the discipline of waiting? Have you received a promise from God but are still waiting for the fulfillment? What was the promise? Share it with a prayer partner or mentor, drawing on his or her faith to support your own.

- Read Romans 8:28-29 out loud. Better yet, memorize it this week. Are there details of your life you need to yield to Jesus? Why not do that now, recording in your journal what the issues are. Later, when you begin to doubt that God is doing something, refer to today's prayer and the journal pages. Thank Him for working everything out according to His will, even if it's a long time coming.

- Reread Galatians 5:22-23. Ask someone very close to you if he or she sees this "fruit of the Spirit" manifested in your life. Which qualities seem to be missing? Then ask that person to pray for areas in your life that need God's pruning and watering.

• Do you know someone who exemplifies the fruit of God's Spirit in his or her everyday life? Write about that person and the impact he or she has had on your life.

• My cousin Betty asked me one day, "What is your song?" The provocative question sent me on a search, some of which is recorded in this chapter. What is *your* song? Write a prayer to God asking Him to reveal your own song—one that's all about Him!

Truth for the Surefooted Journey

Rejoice in the Lord always. I will say it again: Rejoice! Let your gentleness be evident to all. The Lord is near. Do not be anxious about anything, but in everything, by prayer and petition, with thanksgiving, present your requests to God. And the peace of God, which transcends all understanding, will guard your hearts and your minds in Christ Jesus. (Philippians 4:4-7)

Surely God is my salvation;
   I will trust and not be afraid.
The LORD, the LORD, is my strength and my song;
   he has become my salvation.

(Isaiah 12:2)

CHAPTER SIX

UNBURDENING THE BEAST

IT SEEMED LIKE a good idea when we bought the sturdy green suitcase. "It's got a lifetime guarantee, Steve," I persuaded my husband, who studied the costly bag, examining every stitch in its leatherbound frame. "We need to buy one only once."

"Yeah, I know, but can you handle this if I'm not with you?" he asked with concern. Steve had carried the heavy bags for the fifteen years since I'd injured my back.

"Sure! Look! It's got wheels! What could be easier?" Surely this was the perfect solution to my traveling alone when I needed to. That settled it. We bought the bag, and I wheeled it all the way to the car to prove how well I could handle this baby.

The problem came on the very first trip. I crammed it full of clothes and books and left for a weeklong conference in Pennsylvania. Steve was clearly worried. "You can't pick this up, you know. It weighs a ton."

"I know. Don't worry. Someone will pick me up at the airport, and all I'll have to do is roll it over to them. Easy! Watch!" I rolled it around the living room, trying to make it look easy. It wasn't.

Steve was right. I couldn't pick it up. My escort from the airport couldn't, either. We found someone to load it into her van and began the long ride to the college where the conference was being held. Reality hit hard when I realized my room was on the third floor of an old dorm with no elevators. Wheels don't work on stairs, I discovered, along with the fact that many men have back problems, too. When they looked at my big bag, people walked by looking busy. I was nearly in tears. Finally, a skinny, sweet-natured maintenance man showed up and struggled up six flights of stairs — two long flights for each floor — with my immortal green suitcase. I felt like a worm (but a grateful one).

You'd think I'd learn a lesson quickly, but I didn't. More than once I've lifted more than my limit to try to prove I'm not a wuss, only to end up flat on my back again in pain. My pride boasts, "I can handle this. This is nothing. I've been doing this for years" about many of the ridiculous weights I lugged for decades — things like bitterness and blame, a critical spirit, old lies and fears — without realizing those things strained my relationship with God and those I love. My peace of mind suffered as well, along with my enjoyment of daily life and the accomplishment of important goals.

Donkeys are beasts of burden all over the world. They can carry a lot — a whole lot, hundreds of pounds. The problem comes when we attempt to load our little fellow up with useless things we don't need, dead weight that makes our journey and his ridiculously hard. When he starts to sag in the middle, we're sure it's all his fault so we reach for the whip.

How can we dump these burdensome bags? I've found I can't just shake them off. Besides being heavy, they stick like burrs. Each one needs to be removed with care and God's amazing grace.

BLAME

Rehearsing our side of the story so much we almost believe it and blaming others for our problems stop our ears from hearing God's voice. It's like wearing earplugs—His whispers can't get through. It's easy to justify our own hurts and blame our parents, siblings, or lack of social standing or education—anything but take responsibility for ourselves and our reactions.

For years I carried around some heavy "if-only" baggage: "If only I had grown up with a father around." Then one day I had a rude awakening when I asked myself instead, *What if my father had lived? What would life have been like?* Probably not too good, honestly, as his alcoholism and mental health problems created havoc in our home. My brother, Roger, and I were born in between my parents' annual moves all over the Northeast and the South. Eventually, my dad left and finished his last years in a mental institution, dying of a heart attack within five years. Although I loved him greatly, his absence ushered in the first peace our family had known. Possibly his death was God's mercy that left a mark on my heart, making me hunger for a father—a heavenly Father.

There were other good things as well. I learned early to read the emotions in a room when I entered it. *What happened in here before I came in? How are people feeling? Maybe I should just listen or leave quietly.* I still do that. It's proven to be a good skill.

Even though my parents' problems spilled over into my life and my brother's in painful ways, it prepared me well for life and even ministry to others. What a surprise when I realized how well God used those years to equip me to understand hurting people later on, to cope with the challenges our children experienced, to know how to pray others through a tangled mess. How can I blame God or my parents for something He later used for my benefit? We don't always recognize how good something can be until years later.

I think of that now when I'm tempted to wish my family of origin were more like Steve's—loving, humble, openhearted, fun, and faithful. But that's not what God gave me. What He gave me is fine with me now. Without it, I wouldn't be who I am.

BITTERNESS

This could be the twin weight to blame that we load on our donkey. They go together like bulging saddlebags full of old offenses, big and small, gathered over time. The problem is that bitterness smells up everything else when left to rot too long.

Want to know if you are carrying around bitterness? Ask yourself if there is anyone whose name causes you to rehearse a litany of things you don't like about him or her or share critical thoughts disguised as "prayer needs." Is there someone you go to great lengths or expense to avoid? Worse, is there someone whom you've spoken against to others and felt a twinge of conscience?

The phone rang the other day and it was a friend I'll call Janice, whom I had not heard from in a few years. She was open

and direct: "Virelle, I need to talk to you. I need to ask your forgiveness for something that's been bothering me for years."

"Well, suffer no more," I chuckled. "How bad can it be?"

Her voice was pained. "I've held something against you for a
long time. I need to get it off my chest. Maybe we should meet
in person."

"Janice," I answered, her tone sobering me, "it sounds like I
owe you an apology. Tell me now. We'll both feel better if we deal
with it and get it over with."

"Well, okay. I didn't even realize I was nursing hurt feelings
toward you until your name came up in conversation recently
and I heard myself make a disparaging remark about you publicly. I realized it came from an old hurt I hadn't dealt with, and
I want to ask your forgiveness for the bitterness I've been
carrying."

A half hour of healthy, honest, mutual confession ensued.
Janice explained that, in a careless way, I had hurt her through
some poorly timed suggestions regarding her work or ministry.
I barely remembered it, but she was right. How bad I felt to have
caused her pain through my offhand remarks. We asked one
another's forgiveness, and after praying together over the phone,
we both felt a rush of relief. We have since made plans to attend
a conference together, hoping to renew the friendship that was
wounded.

Old hurts, when left to fester, lead to the poison of bitterness. Janice was wise and humble enough to know that confession, loving confrontation, and prayer were the only antidotes.
We both feel lighter now. Unfortunately, no one is exempt from

feeling bitterness and blame. But there is good news: The antidote always works.

REGRET

Aging has its advantages, one of which is hindsight. A few years ago, I decided that for the rest of my life, I want to live without regret. I took a look at some of the junk I was carting around and decided it wasn't worth the weight. Regrets had dragged me down for years; I wanted to see them go.

I argued with myself over some regrets that were just plain stupid, such as not having learned to excel in a sport growing up (*Big deal! Learn now!*) and never having kept baby books for my kids or put all their pictures in albums (*Too late on the baby books. Your kids will have to forgive you. Get busy on the pictures!*). I'm working on it—honestly, I am.

But other regrets were more hidden. They involved people I'd lied to (I once banged up someone's car and told her someone else hit me in the parking lot), been rude to (my poor mother took the heat for all my disappointments growing up), or just plain let down, including myself (that list is too long).

Got a list of regrets? Can I tell you what I did with mine? Burning it would have been too easy. And I couldn't simply say, "Oh, those things don't matter anymore. It's too late now to do anything about them. Move on!" Pop psychology only sounds good; it doesn't work with me. I needed to go deeper and deal with the root, which turned out to be easier than the groveling I dreaded.

I began with a list of my obvious regrets, a few of which I've already mentioned. I went first to the toughest end of the list, the people I had offended in some way. First, I went to my mother and asked her forgiveness. She claimed I never had done anything wrong, which at first I thought was evasive. Now I know that in your late fifties, it's possible to forget almost all the bad things your kids ever did! At least she forgave me. One down. But there were others. Some needed apologies, like the lady whose car I banged up; others needed to be thanked, like my childhood piano teacher, who patiently taught me week after week, even though I seldom practiced.

All in all, it took about a month to cover my regret list and finally throw it away. When I did that, all the donkeys in my life began to look a lot better to me. Had I attached blame to them, too, when I should have owned up to it myself? Yes—more times than I want to confess.

Last, convinced I truly want to live the rest of my life with as small a load of regret as possible (no regrets sounds good, but realistically it's probably impossible for someone like me), here is what I'm aiming for:

1. To be more grateful to God and those around me
2. To praise God more
3. To regard this life as a grand adventure with Him
4. To love those He's given me
5. To never think I'm all done growing up

My friend Bonnie developed the habit of journaling, at the end of each day, five things she was thankful for. She did it every day for a year until the habit was thoroughly ingrained.

She recently told me, "I still practice this habit mentally when I go to bed at night. I'm convinced that rehearsing the things I'm thankful for that day helps me sleep better." What a great way to renew your mind rather than eat your gut!

Wouldn't it be wonderful to live the rest of our lives without dragging around so much dead weight, blaming ourselves or our donkeys for things we can't change, or carrying regret over the things we really do have the power to change? Getting rid of all that baggage leads to true freedom and lightness of spirit. Whew!

WORRY

I never thought I was a worrier until I started really listening to my prayers. I was asking God for the same things all day long, as if He'd never heard me the first time: prayers for Steve's stressful job situation, prayers for my children's health issues, prayers for a mate for one of my sons, prayers for several friends at our church. I would bring up the same things over and over as though I were fingering worry beads. One day, I distinctly sensed God say to me, "Enough!" I didn't know He ever said that about prayer. Isn't prayer the right reflex to stress? What's wrong with praying all day about the same things?

I'm learning it's about balance. Prayers without thanksgiving and praise are better than not praying, but they're only half-said. The other half is saying thank you ahead of time, knowing God heard me and will answer as only He can: perfectly, at just the right time, every time. Worry and anxiety disguised as prayer will drain your soul. Thanking God before the answer comes isn't being manipulative. Who has the power to manipulate the Almighty? It just honors Him and opens our eyes to watching Him act.

Right before Steve became a Christian, our only car died. Steve was a wreck, fussing about how we were ever going to replace it now that another baby, our third, was on the way. I heard a little whisper in my spirit say, "Trust Me on this one. You're going to love how it turns out." So I did. Rather than pray a rocking mantra for a new car, I just said, "Thank You, Lord! I wonder what You have up Your sleeve." He didn't tell me.

The car problem got worse every day. Steve was bumming rides to work with his office mate, Keith, and I was walking to the store for groceries. Just when Steve was about to come unglued, the phone rang. It was a great guy from our church (really *my* church then) who happened to be a car dealer. *Did we want to borrow a car at no cost until we found one?* You bet! That night we had wheels, if only temporary ones. What could be next?

We searched all over Baltimore for a car we could afford that would fit our growing family. Nothing looked very inviting. Then another phone call came from the same man: *Would we be interested in a high-end sedan with fairly high miles? He could make the price very low.* Steve nearly leaped for joy when he saw that beautiful gray low-slung sedan with brocade seats! It was the nicest car we ever owned. And within a very short time, Steve began to think God just might be real after all.

It's so comforting to me to know that God never forgets a matter once I bring it to Him. Long after I've forgotten it, God is still at work. He relishes an invitation to handle our impossibilities.

He's always working on them, even when we see nothing happening for long periods.

If you've dug a well-worn worry rut, there's a way out. Next time you find yourself tapping your fingernails, as I do, or biting your lip or reaching for comfort food to soothe your worries, remember that God is not surprised by your problems or mine. He loves it when we bring them to Him quickly, believing He will answer. Try saying this out loud: "Thank You that You already have the solution to my problem!" You may have to say it ten times a day until your mind agrees with you. And while you're watching and waiting for His answer, listen. He just might speak to you in a completely unexpected way.

TAKING YOURSELF TOO SERIOUSLY

Perhaps you're wondering, *How can this be a weight? Isn't it good to be serious rather than silly?* Only sometimes. Frankly, I prefer silly more often, or at least lighthearted. Someone once said that if people rub you the wrong way, then you ought not to have a wrong way to be rubbed. *Hmmm,* I thought. *What does that mean?* It means that if people often rub me the wrong way, then I'm becoming a regular bore.

Here's a little self-test. Ask yourself, *Am I easily miffed when someone disagrees with my opinion or when I'm ignored and left out? Do I have to be the center of attention or have others notice when I don't feel well or am not happy? Is it important that others consider my particular needs when making plans?* Mind if I tell you they won't?

If you answered "yes" to any of the questions and don't have limiting medical issues, then you're taking yourself too seriously and need to be petted and pleased too much. Spending time with someone like this is a little like going on a hike with a blister on your foot. After a while, it's too much trouble to be worth the effort. The antidote is learning to laugh at yourself a little more. Lighten up!

My friend Lorraine had listened a long time on the phone to my answer to her complex question, "How are you?" It took ten minutes to tell her, after which she sighed and said, "Well, praise the Lord that's over!" *Yes, I guess so,* I admitted to myself. *It is over, and probably not worth talking about anymore.* Only a good friend will tell you something like that. I knew she meant it kindly.

I've learned that it's much better to flip-flop my conversations, first asking what others want, how they feel, what's going on in their lives. Rather than drone on and on about my own concerns (although I sometimes still do), I'm trying to learn to toss the conversation ball back quickly with sincere inquiries, such as "Hey, tell me how you're doing" or "What would you like to do next time we have a free evening?" It's good to aim our thoughts away from our own pressing needs. Why? Because *God* always has us on His mind. He's looking out for our needs before we even ask Him—and He doesn't forget.

ENVY

If you think you're too "spiritual" to be envious, think again. Even the disciples squabbled over who was first, who was greatest, and who would get to sit by Jesus. At the root of envy is the central question "Why not *me?*" It's hard when others soar ahead of us on successful ventures or have bigger houses, thinner bodies, or fatter bank accounts. What's really difficult is when God seems to be blessing their spiritual journey more than ours. Her husband finally came to faith in Jesus. Why not yours? Her kids are all in Christian schools, but yours have no interest. His Bible study group is growing every month. Yours is considering disbanding altogether. Why is that? Is God unfair? Does He play favorites in His family?

When my first book came out thirteen years ago, it wasn't exactly a runaway best seller. But two well-known authors wrote similar books, and guess what? Theirs were. I didn't like those authors for years. Not very nice of me, was it? Have you had someone promoted before you, even though you had the same credentials? It brings out the ugly side of us quickly. Nothing kills a thankful spirit faster than envy.

The fact is, God loves all His children with the same love—the love He has for His Son. It doesn't get any better than that. What He wills for your life is not the same as what He wills for mine or anyone else's. Even though it's not a very satisfying answer, we won't know why until we get to ask Him ourselves. For now, I'd rather be caught cheering for someone else than whining. How about you?

One of the ways God has given me to do that is through my teaching at writers' conferences, helping good writers connect with publishers and encouraging them along the way. I now find great joy helping others succeed.

A COMPLAINING SPIRIT

Listening to a child whine will wear you out no matter how much you love him. It grates, like fingernails on a blackboard. On our nine-thousand-mile, six-week trip across the country when our kids were small, we thought we'd solved the "fighting and whining in the car" problem brilliantly. Each child got five dollars in dimes at the start of the trip. Every fight or complaint cost a ten-cent fine. Anything you didn't lose you could use for fun on the trip home.

The problem was, fifty dimes per kid only got us from New York to Denver. After that, we were on our own. Plus, Steve and I were exempt, which proved not quite fair, either. Why should he be allowed to complain over a little dysentery? All in all, it was a bad system.

Why do I find others' complaining such an odious noise and hardly recognize it from my own mouth? Sometimes complaints are legitimate. Mine certainly are! (Please smile here.) Quite honestly, it's easy to be the whiny child and justify my own complaints, trying to lend them legitimacy. But it's a bad system, too. A better way might be to look myself squarely in the mirror and say, "Oh, be still! If you can't be thankful, at least keep your mouth shut!" Hmmm. Not a bad alternative to whining.

ANGER

There's no sin in being angry once in a while. Try being happy the next time you dump ten cups of hot coffee in the backseat of your new car. I definitely was upset when I did that en route to a board meeting recently.

Anger doesn't become a dead weight until we allow it to hang around too long or call the shots in our temperament and language or block our prayers with bitterness, resentment, and hurt. Then it weighs heavier every hour we carry it.

For years, I had a tough time dumping anger. When the kids would do something wrong, I'd march them up to their rooms, scolding all the way, often giving undeserved spankings. Separating sinful anger from righteous anger (yes, there is "good" anger—the kind Jesus had for the right reasons) seemed impossible to me. Doesn't all anger feel the same? The difference is clearer to me now.

Forgive me if this seems too simple. It's not simple at all, but it is evidence of who is in the driver's seat: God or us. Anger can prove the last hurrah as we relinquish the control of our lives to God. That's why it keeps cropping up. Anger has a lot to do with control and who gets it. The bad kind is slammed into gear by our strong sense of self, especially self-righteousness: *I'm sure I'm right, so nobody better dare get in my way!* Simply said, it never accomplishes anything good. It just makes us feel guilty and miserable and can separate people for a long, long time.

Last summer, our family had the vacation from hell. We all arrived exhausted at the ocean beach house our son had rented as a gift to the family. Our "tanks" were empty emotionally, physically, and probably spiritually. Within twenty-four hours, we were all crabby, careless with each other's feelings, and critical. Guess who started things off? (How did you know that?)

Needless to say, the week got off to a lousy start. It took months, if not the whole following year, to make amends and straighten out hurt feelings—and we are a close family! Very close. All Christians. What happened? It was a question of who was in control.

"Good" anger is quickly submitted to God and serves His purposes, like Jesus ridding the temple of the profiteers with a whip. No one wondered what His motives were. Our anger can also serve a productive purpose, but only when it's under God's control: *Lord, I'm angry! What do You want me to do about this? Help me not to sin.* Even when good anger flares, it's quick to submit to another, ask and give forgiveness, and make amends. It doesn't hold grudges. Healthy anger is so rare that we may exercise it only once or twice in a lifetime—maybe never. Its only motive is to serve God's purposes.

That leaves us with a choice again, today and every day: Will we submit the whole of our personality, defects and all, to God? If so, let's get to work on unloading this burro one weight at a time and expect to hear God better than ever before.

Face to Face

- Can you relate to my plight with the bulging green suitcase? Unloading the foolish weights we carry is very freeing. Take a look inside your own bag. (Warning: This may not be pretty.) List each weight and try approximating how long each one has been there. By the way, the reason they are called "dead weights" is that, over time, they deaden our enjoyment of life, cripple our spirit, dry up our strength, and silence our song.

- Ready to dump your weights now? Here's what helped me. First, I prayerfully gave each one to God, asking Him to carry them or discard them and set me free. Next, I wrote that day's date next to each weight I gave Him. Whenever I felt myself shouldering a certain weight again, I could point at that date and say, "No, Virelle—you gave this up, remember? Put it down and get busy with something far better, like thankfulness, praise, and doing the next thing God gives you to do." Try this process yourself.

- Is your weight busyness? It seems like a good thing at first, until you wake up one morning, look at your calendar, and can hardly breathe. Cynthia Heald records her own personal struggle with busyness in her book *Abiding in Christ.* Talking about the pruning process God uses to help us recognize needed changes, she says:

*God wants to cut back the nonessentials in our lives
so that we will be more able to draw our life from one
source—the Vine. This process can be painful, but it
is always for our good. As we yield to God's loving
desire to strip or sever the extraneous twigs and
branches in our lives, we will learn endurance and
trust. Increasingly, this develops within us a calm and
patient spirit—the evidence of His fruit in our lives.*[1]

I trust Cynthia. Over the past ten years or so, she has
become a friend and mentor to me as a writer and speaker.
About a year ago, we had dinner together. I shared with her
my confusion over which direction God wanted me to pro-
ceed: with radio, writing, speaking, or all three. She smiled at
me and said, "Virelle, all I can tell you is what Philippians
3:13 says: 'But *one* thing I do . . .' You are doing too much.
Ask God to show you the way." And, of course, He did. Within
months, my radio show was canceled due to financial adjust-
ments at our corporate offices, and I had a new book contract
and a quiet life. Hallelujah!

Does anything need pruning in your busy life? Do you
dare ask God to prune your activities? Ask your best friend
or mentor to help you discern what needs to go. What a
happy relief it is to spend our talents wisely!

• There are weights that call for the help of an outside counselor
  or pastor, such as the wounding of abuse, depression, and

addictions. Wise people don't hesitate to seek godly counselors. If you feel the need, make an appointment today.

• Write a prayer of response to God, thanking Him for leading you in the process of rediscovering joy and freedom.

Truth for the Surefooted Journey

If we claim to be without sin, we deceive ourselves and the truth is not in us. If we confess our sins, he is faithful and just and will forgive us our sins and purify us from all unrighteousness. (1 John 1:8-9)

I do not consider myself yet to have taken hold of it. But one thing I do: Forgetting what is behind and straining toward what is ahead, I press on toward the goal to win the prize for which God has called me heavenward in Christ Jesus. All of us who are mature should take such a view of things. (Philippians 3:13-15)

CHAPTER seven

LETTING GOD HANDLE THE HERD

I HAD THE wrong idea. Totally. Often when a donkey moved into my life, I would think, *This is a new project sent from God! He must want me to manage this burro well, lead it to drink, feed it regularly, and take good care of it. This baby is now my responsibility.* That assumption has caused major problems when God had a different agenda entirely.

Your donkey may be on your doorstep right now, looking like a close friend or family member whose pressing needs spill over into your life regularly. Whether physical, emotional, financial, or relational (or possibly all of them combined), the predicament is the same: Love, or at least deep concern, rises in your heart daily like the tide. Surely, God must want you to *do something*, be the good Samaritan. But what, exactly, can and should you do?

It's the struggle of every caregiver or parent of unsettled or handicapped adult children. Or perhaps it's a needy friend, sibling, widowed or divorced parent, or elderly family member whose needs cause you to worry about his or her well-being and feel burdened with a sense of responsibility.

When these very personal donkeys arrive at our doorsteps or plop themselves in the middle of our living rooms, what are we to do? Step into the role of "fixer," part-time Savior, intermittent Holy Spirit? If we do, we step into a role God never intended: His own. We end up shutting ourselves in the same corral as our donkey, and over time we fear there is no way out for either of us.

LETTING GOD BE GOD

While browsing in a gift shop last fall, I ran into a woman about my age looking at Christmas cards. She seemed a friendly sort, and I struck up a conversation with her immediately.

"My grandkids would love the snowmen on this card," I said. "They're from the South and are coming home for Christmas. I want to make a snowman with them." (We never got to do it because the three feet of "holiday" snow didn't fall until the day after they left!)

She sighed and then looked at me with her eyes full of tears. "I never get to see my grandchildren," she said. "They live in California."

"I don't understand," I answered. "Why couldn't you visit them for the holidays?"

She shook her head and looked away. "I have my parents here. We can't leave them alone on Christmas. I wouldn't do that."

Stunned speechless, I had no response, because for too many years this woman was me.

Everything I wanted to tell her I couldn't say without being a hypocrite: *You owe it to yourself, to your husband, and especially to your kids in California to be with them, too! Don't try to play God, making your parents happy all the time, fixing everything. You'll stand in His way. Besides, it's unfair to all the others who love you.* Instead, I just walked away, replying softly, "I'm sorry to hear that, but I wish you'd go anyway. Your kids will miss you."

"I know," was all she said.

Out in the afternoon sun, I walked past store after store, lost in thought. It had taken so long for me to let God be God in my mother's life, to stop trying to arrange things so she would finally be happy after a life of great hardship.

Over and over, she has told my brother and me the stories of her childhood in Cincinnati: about her brilliant but emotionally distant father, her tenderhearted mother, her doting older brothers. The lights of my mother's life went out when she was only nineteen or twenty: Her father died of a sudden heart attack and then her mother died of cancer six months later.

After putting herself through college during the Depression, losing the family home, and living in semipoverty, she met my charismatic, fun-loving father and married him within three months. Less than a year went by before his alcoholism and untreated mental illness drove her to the edge of her depleted resources. She chose sheer grit to survive.

I loved my father, but as a young child, I had once prayed he would die rather than cause my mother to suffer anymore. When he did, I felt responsible for his death and shouldered the burden to make up for all her unhappy years. God knows how hard I tried, but I couldn't do it anymore. I was miserable, and my mother was no better off.

Finally, I went to see a counselor, desperate for relief from the incredible burden I had carried for more than forty years. The counselor's words aimed right at the heart of the issue: "Virelle, are you trying to please God, or your mother? You can't do both."

Why not? I thought. *Wasn't that one of the main reasons God brought us back to Albany, to give my mother happiness and support in her later years after a life of suffering and hardship?*

"Isn't that what a daughter does for her parents?" I asked. "Take care of them?"

"No," he said simply. "Not if it means putting them ahead of her husband, family, ministry, and personal health and well-being. Being a loving daughter doesn't mean that. It means honoring God by honoring your mother as a person He loves, by caring about her concerns as you would for your own but not taking care of all her needs and not interfering with her decisions, even if you don't agree with them. You can't make other people happy; that's God's responsibility and theirs. By stepping in to fix everything, you are preventing your mother from seeking God's help, from fully depending on Him for the wisdom she needs to make decisions about her own life."

I started to cry. *Could relief be this simple?* I thought incredulously. How long had I been my mother's burden-bearer and trail guide, trying everything I could think of to handle her needs and "help" her find the happiness and peace of mind I longed for her to enjoy? For as long as I could remember. I'm sure my mother never intended for me to feel this way. I just took on the role because I thought that's how good Christian daughters were supposed to act.

"Baloney," said my counselor, with a gentle smile. He handed me a box of tissues while I laughed and cried simultaneously at the unexpected voice of relief. Imagine life without tons of guilt! My husband and kids had also sacrificed so much to help me carry this burden of "ought-tos" and "have-tos." They seldom complained when it meant missing countless family occasions over the years because I was just like the woman in the gift shop.

Facing that truth was hard. I had assumed a role in my mother's life that God had never assigned me. What He asked of me was to show His love, not handle His business. My mother's happiness is now, and always was, in His hands and hers, not mine.

Are you in a similar situation with someone you love? Is your frequent prayer, "Lord, what about my brother or sister? My child? My dear friend? The needs of my parents or spouse? What about . . . ?" (You fill in the blank.) How does God want us to express His love and care? I wish I had a one-size-fits-all answer, but I don't, of course. Only through face-to-face encounters with our living, loving God can each of us discover what He wants of us. That's what donkeys on a God-mission do: They lead us to seek and find our answers and our consolation in God alone. Only He can give us everything we need on our journey. And only He can handle the rest of His herd.

It should not surprise us, then, when God asks us to hand back to Him the needs and desires of those with whom our lives are intertwined. It will mean letting go, something we are rarely eager to do. When we place the well-being of another soul into the hands of an all-loving and all-powerful God, the cost of that surrender feels at first like sacrifice. It may even feel cruel, wrong, and utterly unloving to the person we've been God to for so long. How can we stop? How do we love without meddling or managing? What if our loved one gets angry? What if he or she says terrible things about us to others?

"So what?" is the question I am learning to ask. If God is not impressed, does it matter if anyone else is? If you or I experience years of disfavor with others, if we suffer unfairly for doing the right thing, we have lots of good company. The reward is worth it: freedom. Not freedom from serving, helping, loving, and praying, but freedom from bearing burdens not intended for our only-human shoulders, freedom from false guilt, freedom to do and become whatever God calls us to do or be.

For me, there have been some additional and unexpected benefits of this kind of letting go. I'm enjoying a more honest relationship with my mother in the late winter of her life. She is not the "queen" anymore; rather, she is a fellow subject of the King of kings, who loves us both beyond measure. It's not always easy, but Steve and I now have far less trouble than before spending a holiday with his family or with our out-of-town kids. We are healthier emotionally and relationally, and life feels so much better.

Do you feel trapped in the middle of a herd of braying donkeys? (I've found that even one that brays loud enough can sound like a whole herd!) What would you do if you were free? How would your life be different? How might you feel?

There's a secret place, I've discovered, where God welcomes

donkeys that need special attention from Him. You and I can't go into that place, but through prayer and letting go we can play an important role in leading needy donkeys there for safekeeping by the One who loves them perfectly.

THE KEEPING ROOM

I first found it one morning quite by accident, or so it seemed, in one of Mrs. Charles Cowman's classic devotionals, *Springs in the Valley*. It was a room I would visit again and again and has become for me a place of miracles. Come with me on a short journey in Scripture (see 2 Kings 4)[1] to meet a woman who taught me the way to the "Keeping Room," a holy place filled with God's power.

You may know her as the Shunammite woman. Let's call her Ariel. She was a well-to-do woman who used her resources to help others. People loved being in her home, eating at her well-laden table. God's prophet Elisha was no exception.

Ariel and her husband insisted Elisha join them for a meal whenever he passed through their town near Galilee. One day she said to her husband, "Why don't we build him his own room on the roof to use whenever he needs it? I can fix it up with a bed and a chair and a table with an oil lamp. I'll make it nice for him." Her husband gladly agreed: "Consider it done!"

Ariel found joy in caring for others. Some people thought she had everything—a big house, servants, a good crop every year—but Elisha knew better. Ariel also had a broken heart. Long ago she had given up her dream of ever bearing a child.

Now that her husband was along in years, it seemed far too late to hold out hope. They found ways to love other people's children instead.

One day, Elisha said to his servant Gehazi, "Go to this wonderful Shunammite woman and say, 'You have been so kind to us. What can we do for you? Perhaps a word to bring you favor with the king?'" Naturally, she declined.

Then Gehazi had an idea of his own, realizing the woman had no son and her husband was old: A baby! What a perfect gift!

"Call her," Elisha said excitedly. So Gehazi went to get her, and Ariel came and stood in the doorway. "Around this time next year," Elisha announced, "you will hold a son in your arms."

To Ariel, it seemed almost cruel at first. But surely Elisha, the man of God, wouldn't deceive her so. I picture her framed in the day's waning light, hardly able to speak. "No, my lord," she objected. "Don't mislead me." Ariel had asked, wept, begged, prayed for years for this blessing—and nothing had happened. Now Elisha was zeroing in on her deepest longing when it seemed far too late to be fulfilled. His good news was too much to take in, too wonderful. Dare she believe it possible?

An eleventh-hour miracle was on its way. "The next year about that same time she gave birth to a son, just as Elisha had told her" (2 Kings 4:17). That would be a lovely end to the story if they all lived happily ever after. But that's not what happened.

The story escalated dramatically when the child was old enough to accompany his father to the fields where he supervised the reapers. Suddenly, the boy cried out in pain, "My head! My head!"

"Quick!" his father yelled to a servant. "Carry him to his mother!"

I picture Ariel working in the kitchen preparing the evening meal. Looking out the window she sees a figure rushing toward the house carrying a bundle of some sort. The bundle is her son, her precious child! Dropping her tasks, she rushes to meet him and gathers the limp little boy in her arms.

"Oh, my son, my sweet son," she coos, sitting down on a garden bench, rocking him gently and singing softly to him. Caressing his head, Ariel silently begs God for help, but none comes. At noon, her dream dies in her arms.

From this tragic moment, Ariel's deliberate actions speak volumes to me. Quietly, she carried her dead child to Elisha's upper chamber. There she "laid him on the bed of the man of God, then shut the door and went out" (verse 21). *Wait a minute. She went out? How did she do that? Just laid down her dead son, walked out, and shut the door?* Ariel could do that because she knew what I need to know: There is no better place for those we love than in the presence of God. Elisha's room was the closest place she knew to His presence. But she didn't stop there. She had to speak directly with the man who spoke for God. "She called her husband and said, 'Please send me one of the servants and a donkey so I can go to the man of God quickly and return'" (verse 22). Soon she found Elisha at Mount Carmel.

Stop for a moment and consider this picture. Here is a godly woman known to have received the best gift of all from God: a beloved son. Now he is suddenly and inexplicably taken away. She could have run sobbing to her husband, relatives, and friends, but instead she went straight to the source of the promise — straight to the man of God — with her broken dreams.

It's significant to me that she rode on a donkey, as did Abraham climbing the mountain to sacrifice Isaac and as did Balaam on his way to the king. Our donkeys today are not just fuzzy gray animals with quiet natures and long soft ears; they are life's burden-bearers, carrying us to a place of extremity in our faith journey where we will meet God face-to-face.

Upon reaching Elisha, Ariel fell at his feet in bitter distress, weeping out the sad tale of her son's death. "'Did I ask you for a son, my lord?' she said. 'Didn't I tell you, "Don't raise my hopes"?'" (verse 28).

Elisha immediately ordered Gehazi to rush to the child's side and lay Elisha's staff on the child's face. But Ariel would settle for nothing other than Elisha returning home with her. Having been persuaded, he went. Although Gehazi had done as Elisha had asked, the boy had not stirred by the time the prophet arrived. So Elisha entered the room and shut the door on both Ariel and Gehazi.

Can you imagine waiting on the quiet side of the door, anticipating what's happening in there? Ariel's faith is a marvel to me. I have asked myself many times how she waited outside without knowing the outcome, having relinquished all control, yielding her dearest and her best. It was enough for her that her son was in the presence of God's anointed servant.

Ariel had far less to go on than you and I in terms of faith. We have Jesus, the proof of God's active, saving grace! We have His Holy Spirit living in our hearts and continual access to God through prayer and His living Word. One day as I considered the Shunammite woman's example and my own situation with my mother and others whose needs weighed heavily on my heart, I thought, *Why can I not carry those I love into the sanctuary of God's power and love, lay them down at Jesus' feet, and then leave in His divine safekeeping my broken dreams and the lives of those closest to me?*

I *can* do that, I've discovered, with prayer. I started a new page in my journal that day, titling it "The Keeping Room." At first I listed only one or two names. Now I have at least a dozen who have been ushered inside. As I lay them down in God's presence, my prayer for each one is simple: "Lord, here is one I love and You love. I leave him in Your keeping, asking that Your best will be done in his life. I release him to You with great thanks and praise for all You will do, even if I am not privileged to see it. Keep him, Lord, in the strong name of Jesus. Amen."

The liberation that prayer of surrender brings is amazing. When I pray it sincerely, anxiety and concern no longer hold me in their viselike grip. Suddenly I can breathe easier. The one I love is now God's responsibility entirely. I am free, released, ready to serve Him however He directs. If God continues to keep me in a role of love and service to their needs, so be it. I can do that gladly, as I would serve Jesus Himself. But the outcome is out of my hands and into His. Blessed relief!

The problem for me comes on the quiet side of the door. I want to peek through the keyhole and see what Jesus is doing in there, even pass notes under the door: "How's it going in there? Need any help? Lord, I have a great idea for You! You may not have thought of this." But He never answers. He just continues His work without letting me know what He's doing. And that's as it should be.

Ariel, the bereaved mother, received her son back alive. Incalculable joy! A resurrection gift impossible for anyone but God to give, just as He had placed her child in her womb in the first place. I believe that God does His most amazing work when we commit our loved ones to His care in the Keeping Room. Even those who were once dead to Him can receive new life, those who have been wounded by life can be healed, and those who need His redeeming touch can experience it as intimately as Ariel's son experienced the presence of Elisha.

Do you know the best thing about the Keeping Room? The stories that come out of it are all about what God does—not what we do—in that room. Only He can perform such miracles. All we do is pray and surrender those we love to God's care.

I believe the greatest campfire stories in heaven will come from that room. When we finally take our hands off other people's lives and release them to God, we give them freedom to deal with God face-to-face. No more coercion by us; no more "fixing." God doesn't need our help after all. He just needs our love, our faith, and our trust.

Yielding to God our dearest and our best is a high form of worship that honors Him in a holy way. Will you do that? One by one, in prayer, will you give to God each person over whom you feel responsibility, even anguish? Will you trust Him to do what is best, even if you don't get to see the answer to your prayers for many years or until heaven?

This may sound easy, even simplistic at first. Trust me, I know it isn't. Many times, I have revisited the Keeping Room page in my journal to remind myself that God is in control now, not me. Over time, I am learning to thank and praise Him way ahead of His answers. Expect your resolve to be tested again and again. Even today, I have to consciously take my "fix-it" hands off my mother's life, especially when I disagree with her choices. I don't expect God to call on me to use my voice to show her anything; He's perfectly capable of doing that Himself.

As contrary as it is to our human nature, God is working out His nature in yours and mine, which includes a graciousness and trust in the midst of uncertainty and difficulty, something totally divine. Do we trust Him or not? Letting God handle the herds in our lives is a good place to show Him we do.

Face to Face

• Have you felt hemmed in by someone else's needs or desires? Did my story about playing God in my mother's life strike a chord in your own? Women are often tenderhearted and empathetic by nature. Many of us take on others' burdens without even being asked. The trouble is, God never gave us that role. He is the Savior, the Healer, the Counselor, and the Deliverer. The best thing we can do for others is pray for them, love them, serve them when God directs, and point them to Jesus. We are not equipped to fix their problems or make them happy.

Rather than feel excessive guilt right now over people whose burdens press in on you, why not write out a prayer for them and for you? Ask God to fill their lives with unmistakable evidence of His power and love, and then ask Him to give you a healthier focus.

• Letting go is very difficult. Catherine Marshall's book *Beyond Ourselves* has helped me many times over the years. One chapter I return to again and again is "The Prayer of Relinquishment," a bold and courageous form of prayer in which we release to God the outcome we so long for. It's not prayer for sissies or the strong-willed; it's prayer with more meekness than muscle, more surrender than strength.

Catherine, bedridden for months with an unexplained illness, relates her own struggles to let go of her unanswered prayers:

God was trying to teach me something important about prayer. Still I got only part of the message. I saw that the demanding spirit—"God, I must have thus and so; God, this is what I want You to do for me"—is not real prayer and hence receives no answer. I understood that the reason for this is that God absolutely refuses to violate our free will and that therefore, unless self-will is voluntarily given up, even God cannot move to answer prayer.[2]

It was not until she finally gave up totally, tears flowing, spirit and body broken, saying, "I'm beaten, finished. God, You decide what You want for me the rest of my life"[3] that healing began.

Why? I'm not sure I know, but I'm finding that the crisis of faith that leads to the prayer of relinquishment forges deeper intimacy with God. He is our only consolation. His is the answer; His is the miracle to give. Our part is to rest in His love and release others to His safekeeping.

Have your prayers for someone or some situation gone unanswered? Follow the Shunammite woman's example. Leave your loved ones and your dreams inside the Keeping Room, where God's presence and power can work miracles— even if they are only in your own heart. Look fear and false guilt in the face and say, "God, I trust You to do what is best, even if it's not what I'm asking for. Use me, or not, as You choose." (No peeking under the door; no knocking to see if He's done. It may be quiet for a long, long time.) Now tell God, "Here I am, Lord. What's next for You and me?" Let Him refuel your spirit as you look to Him with fresh expectancy.

Truth for the Surefooted Journey

My heart is not proud, O LORD,
  my eyes are not haughty;
I do not concern myself with great matters
  or things too wonderful for me.
But I have stilled and quieted my soul;
  like a weaned child with its mother,
  like a weaned child is my soul within me.
(Psalm 131:1-2)

You will keep in perfect peace
  him whose mind is steadfast,
  because he trusts in you.
(Isaiah 26:3)

chapter eight

The Guide Within

EACH OF US, at some point, must answer the same question: *Will I saddle up the donkeys that come my way and cooperate with the way God is leading me?* If not, we will fight with Him all our lives, maybe even end up dumping our faith. I know plenty of people who have done that, crusting over their rebellion with a self-righteous, judgmental veneer. If you meet them in their later years, there's very little substance or joy left inside. Their souls dry up and rattle like old gourds.

But if we do welcome the donkeys God allows; relinquish the anger, blame, and control that make up our human nature; let go of the whip once disguised as anxious and demanding prayers; and turn to look God full in the face, listening with a humble heart, a vastly altered landscape opens before us. The hurdles remain, but the rewards ahead are sweet: ears tuned to God's whispered guidance, a rich and unhindered prayer life, increasing recognition of God's fingerprints all over the details of the journey, the peace that accompanies His hands on the reins, and a shared adventure pursuing His highest purposes.

The call to ride with God is unparalleled by any other call in life. Even so, completing this journey requires more than a willing spirit on our parts. We need all of God at work in all of us, one day at a time.

LOVED AND LIFTED HIGH

In my memory bank are a few mental pictures I savor. One involves both my mother and father taking me on a shopping trip to the "big city" of Syracuse, New York. We had just moved for no particular reason to the small upstate town of Mexico, about forty-five minutes north of Syracuse. My father just liked the town when we drove through it on vacation. That was it— he had to move. Moving was an annual event for our family.

I was about six—small enough to get tired easily, but big enough to be out with my parents all day. I'm not sure where my eleven-year-old brother was. Perhaps he walked on ahead by himself, as he usually did. I held both my parents' hands in the spring sun as we walked down the city streets. At each curb, they would lift me high off the cement and yell, "Wheee!" This happened a good ten times. My shoulders strained with each swinging lift, but I didn't care. We were laughing together. It was the last fun moment I remember having with them before the darkness closed in and my father left.

I'm so glad my parents gave me that gift. Today I recall the happy feeling of being lifted high over the big curbs. Peter must have felt something similar when he set out to meet Jesus on the water (see Matthew 14:25-33)[1]:

"Lord, if it's really you," he called to the moonlit figure walking toward him, "tell me to come out to meet You!"

"Come, Peter!" Jesus smiled encouragement, extending both arms. The exuberant Peter jumped out of the boat and walked toward Jesus on the waves. *The waves! What am I doing?* He suddenly regarded the whirling water at his feet.

"Master, save me! I'm going to drown!"

Jesus' firm grip was instantaneous. Helping Peter climb back into the boat, He chided gently, "Hey, my faint-hearted friend, what got into you? Why did you doubt me?"

Without divine power, mere humans can't walk on water, of course. We get frozen with fear that God might not come through for us, that He might look away for a moment and not see us going down like a lead pipe. But Jesus had His eye on Peter all the time, as He does on you and me. Lifted high when he might have sunk, never forgotten for a moment, Peter was the object of his Savior's loving attention. "Wheee!" Peter could walk on water. So can we. With every storm that comes, we are lifted high when we look to Jesus' abiding presence within.

Jesus planned way ahead of time to help us make it safely over every stormy sea and down every rugged canyon. He knew riding life's donkeys would be impossible without Him. That's why He said:

> *"Live in me. Make your home in me just as I do in*
> *you. In the same way that a branch can't bear*
> *grapes by itself but only by being joined to the vine,*
> *you can't bear fruit unless you are joined with me.*
> *"I am the Vine, you are the branches. When*
> *you're joined with me and I with you, the relation*

intimate and organic, the harvest is sure to be abun-
dant. Separated, you can't produce a thing." (John
15:4-5, MSG)

What does this mean for me today? It means when Jesus
lifts me up from within, I can leap over any hurdle in my path.
So can you.

QUESTIONS NOT WORTH ASKING

I used to wonder what it would have been like if I'd lived out my
dream to be an interpreter at the UN (an idea that lost its luster
quickly in college) or if we'd lived somewhere else to raise our
family. What a waste of mental energy! Now I know that God was
guiding our choices all the time, never forcing us to let Him lead
but rather extending His hand to hold the reins if we'd let Him.
He reached out for us at every turn in the road and always
wanted to talk with us on the way. The "intimate and organic"
relationship with Jesus is found only in the shared journey—
lifting, leaning, talking, listening, laughing, crying—all face-to-
face with the One who calls us beloved. The experiences we share
make up the story of our life together, one we never expected, but
a story that is all about Him and His redeeming love.

Many years ago, as a new believer, I attended a picnic in
Baltimore sponsored by our local Christian women's club. I
brought a family friend, an unhappy teenager named Melissa,
who needed a break from her family. Our home became the
respite she needed. As I progressed through a difficult preg-

nancy, Melissa became the angel we needed who eventually ran our whole busy household.

The picnic was held on the sweeping lawns of someone's home, where twenty or more women milled around setting outdoor tables and arranging food. I noticed a pretty blond girl in a wheelchair, laughing and talking in a cluster of women. On the back of her wheelchair were the words "The Lord is my Shepherd."

Melissa and I seated ourselves at the far end of the picnic table, feeling awkward about sitting too close to the wheelchair girl. I had watched her long enough to realize that she was a quadriplegic. *What if she needs help eating?* I thought. *I wouldn't know how to offer, and she'd be embarrassed to have strangers help her.* It soon became clear that she could manage very well eating on her own with the braces that supported her paralyzed arms. *She's really amazing!* I thought. *I wonder who she is.*

I soon found out. Four years after she had broken her neck in a diving accident, Joni Eareckson was our speaker for the evening. She would one day become a famous author, artist, speaker, and radio host with a worldwide ministry. Now, over thirty years later, I remember nearly every word she said. Joni freely admitted she would still like to be able to walk, dress herself, ride a horse, swim, and run. Then she said, "I thank God every day for allowing me to break my neck. I've learned more in four years about Christ than most people do in their lifetime."

Something inside me screamed, *How can she say that? How is that possible?* The more she spoke about her faith in Christ, the more I realized none of her words were cotton-candy fluff. As a very young woman, Joni had endured what many would call a living hell, spending months in a Striker frame in a rehab center, losing her boyfriend (and possibly future husband), taking months to learn small skills using only a few intact neck and shoulder muscles, and accepting the excruciating reality that she would never walk or live normally again or bear children. How could she be thankful for *that?*

Even though it sounded too good to be true, I believed what Joni said about her journey of faith, and so did my teenage friend. Just like Joni, Melissa had struggled with depression and disillusionment. She fantasized about how life could have been so different had she been raised in another family or behaved better in her own. Just as Joni longed for a life full of adventure and romance, so did Melissa. But Joni was happy and free, even though she was bound to a wheelchair. Melissa was healthy, strong, and miserable.

As Joni talked about listening to God's voice calling us to Him, my young friend's heart began to open. We arrived home later that night, and Melissa spent the next three days reading a Bible and asking questions. I answered the best I could. Then one morning, she came into the kitchen, brushed her long dark hair away from her face, and smiled. She said softly, "I asked Jesus into my heart last night."

Yielding our lives to the Lord's control and loving guidance is the most unnatural thing to do, but when it's authentic, like Joni's faith-filled surrender was, we become magnets for drawing others to Jesus. His power is loosed when our needs are greatest.

Your donkey may not be as challenging to ride as Joni's, but it is carrying you to the same place, where you will need Jesus—His power, strength, and love—within you every day. Tackling any God-sized work—whether it's caring for an invalid husband, coping with a rebellious teenager, rebuilding a marriage, dealing with a difficult boss, managing a chronic illness, or carrying a heavy workload without neglecting our relationships—is possible only when God lives powerfully inside us.

The problem is, inside me can be a stormy place where turmoil threatens to whip up waves of anger, resentment, and rebellion. Sometimes peace, gratitude, strength, and faith seem far out of reach. Still, Jesus asks me to come to Him on the rough water and trust Him to hold me up. When I let Him rule within my heart as well as in my circumstances and relationships, I experience the Spirit-led life He promises to everyone who calls Him Lord.

SPIRIT-FILLED AND SPIRIT-LED

Many years ago, I stood in a group of hundreds of other Christians as Bill Bright taught a series of messages that would radically alter my Christian life. I knew Jesus had come into my heart several years earlier. I also understood that the Holy Spirit had entered my life at that time to "seal" me as a believer, to offer me the fullness of Christ's presence and power within. The problem was, I didn't always "feel" Him there. I was often still a mess inside—critical, complaining, unhappy. How could that be?

Dr. Bright explained that the filling of the Holy Spirit means giving Jesus His rightful place as Lord of our lives and yielding control to Him so that we are Christ-centered rather than self-centered. He explained the concept of "spiritual breathing"—regularly, even instantly, confessing sin to God as soon as we recognize it, like we would spit out poison, and then asking Him to cleanse us and fill us again with the Holy Spirit. It made sense.

When the question "Are you ready to be filled with the Holy Spirit?" was asked, the entire crowd stood, me among them. Could it be this simple? We prayed as one to be filled by faith, filled like the rush of air into waiting lungs, filled by asking and receiving the fullness of Christ Himself.

For me there was no fanfare, no dramatic manifestations of the Spirit's indwelling—just peace, assurance, trust, and excitement. What did God have for me next? With His Lordship clearly established, now I could leap over high hurdles with Him, walk on water, and ride my donkeys with confidence and grace! Dr. Bright made it sound so easy. I could hardly wait to go home.

What a letdown that was! I walked in the door expecting life to feel different, but the same people were inside my house! They hadn't changed at all. For all of five minutes I felt peaceful. Then one of the kids mentioned he needed to be dropped off at soccer practice right now, another was hungry and wanted to know what was for dinner, my husband was busy changing the oil on the car, and on and on. You get the picture. Where was the new, amazing, Spirit-filled Virelle, able to leap tall buildings, tackle problems with ease, and pray without ceasing? She was nowhere to be found. Apparently, *I* hadn't changed either.

Had *God* failed? Had *I?* Over the years, I'm continuing to learn what the Spirit-led life is and what it isn't. It isn't the absence of feelings of frustration, hurt, or anger. It isn't the absence of conflict, worry, or anxiety. It isn't knowing all the answers to everyone's problems, including my own. It's real life, but it's the best life there is because Jesus is lifting me, guiding me from within, talking to me, and listening—all the time. He freely offers me wisdom and strength for every situation; I only need to ask. Best of all, He loves me whether I fail or not, whether I pay attention to His voice or not. He never stops loving me and never leaves. Never.

Jesus knows that life can be stressful, hurtful, or just too busy. He knows that the demands people make are draining, that finances can be tight, that death and sorrow come to all. He knows our feet can feel leaden with dread or resistance at times. He knows all about how we feel inside, our weaknesses, our strengths. He knows our faith is small, but *He* isn't. When a new donkey is braying outside our door, He offers us His right hand to hold the reins, keeps our donkey from stumbling, and leads us steadily through each day with unnatural joy and confidence. No problem is too big, no sorrow too deep. He is both our front and rear guard, and nobody gets the jump on Jesus.

I don't have to feel spiritual all the time to know I am. Unless He checks my spirit with that little nudge of caution, I don't have to feel God guiding me to know that He is. And He never looks away. His eye is on His children all the time, watching and cheering us on every moment.

HONORING OUR FATHER

The longer I know God and love Him, the simpler that being a Christian gets. Quite the opposite of what I once thought! Another family memory helps me see my relationship with Him in bold relief.

One gorgeous Saturday in May when our boys, Dave and Bob, were about eight and nine, they both ran in their first road race. It was a special event for each grade level at the elementary school. The kids were nervous and beyond excited. It also happened to be their dad's birthday.

"Just do your best, guys," Steve said. "You can do it!"

Bang! The first mob of third-grade boys burst forth from the starting line, tore around a wide circle in the parking lot, and headed toward the finish line in front of the school. Right out in front was Bob's dandelion-blond head, bouncing far ahead of the pack. As he pumped red-faced across the finish line, his long thin legs flying, he beamed at his dad. First place over all the third-grade boys!

"You made it, Bob! You won!" Steve cheered.

Then, bang! Instantly the fourth-grade boys charged down the same course, grunting and huffing with all the bravado they could muster, being of course, one year older and certainly faster. There was Dave, neck and neck with a bigger boy. It looked as though the other boy would outdo him, but in a surge of strength, Dave kicked his stride a little longer and won. Two first-place winners in one family on the same day!

For a moment, both boys cradled the first trophies they had ever won. Then they walked over to their dad and gave him the trophies. "Here, Dad. Happy birthday!"

"Guys," Steve said, tearing up, "you don't have to do that! It was enough just to see you run, just to cheer you on." But they insisted, and their gifts were added to our house of treasures.

What a moment to remember! It never happened again. There were lots of other victories for each of our four children, and losses, too—some very personal. But they always knew that their dad and mom were cheering them on, lifting them when needed, praying for them and believing in them. We have watched our children get up and keep running their life races when discouragements threatened to make them falter or fall. Each one is a hero to us now.

I think God looks at us much the same. He cheers us on, saying, "Keep on doing your best, child. I am so pleased with you!" And when we stumble or fall, especially then, we honor God by reaching out for His help once again.

I'm growing up a bit now. I wake up more often with a song of thanksgiving rather than a list of needs: *Thank You, God, for allowing me to live for You today! Thank You that You guide me with Your eye on me all the time as I ride the donkeys in my life in a way that honors You. Thank You for choosing me to be Your child, for loving me. Give me someone to love in Your name today. Do You see my smile, Lord? I'm smiling at You as I ride. Help me ride my best for You through this day.*

WORSHIPING ALL THE WAY

People and problems may drain us; there's no sin in that. Jesus felt the same way. But worship fills us, as it filled Him, too. Often in the early-morning hours, Jesus sought time with His Father alone on the hillside. He worshiped and prayed, filling up with His heavenly Father's strength for whatever the day would hold (see Mark 1:35). Hunger for His Father's love drew Jesus to seek Him. Have you ever wondered why? If Jesus, God incarnate, still needed daily discourse with the One who sent Him on His mission, you can be sure we do, too. Yet, how silly we are when we reduce worship and prayer to mere principles or practices. I wonder how that makes God feel.

When our children were young, I often felt guilty if I overslept through my morning time with the Lord. So often we'd be up in the night with a sick child or just overtired, and pretty soon it was morning and a little face was by our bed looking hungry. *Rats! Missed again, Lord. I'm sorry.* Now there are no children living at home and I still oversleep sometimes, but without the guilt. Why? Because the Holy Spirit never sleeps! It's Christ's indwelling strength I borrow daily—His joy, His faith, His wisdom, and His love. When I come to Him with arms outstretched, He gives Himself to me freely all day as I ask Him to fill me with His Spirit and worship Him with a thankful heart. I make time to sit and listen to Him and talk with Him out of love now, not just discipline. The Spirit has set me free.

So how does the Guide within help me when a new challenge arrives, a donkey waiting to carry me further on the path

God has mapped out for me? Jesus says simply, "Come this way, child, and I will meet with you. Listen closely. I have something important to tell you that you've never heard before." I know better now after three decades of following hard after God that the Guide within can be trusted. Even though it's not always easy, He enables me to smile at Him in genuine love and trust and say, "Yes, Lord. Whatever You want."

But, what's this? Climbing into the saddle, I notice something wonderful about this donkey that I hadn't seen before. It is marked with a cross on its back. (They all are, you know.) Amazing! I wonder if God paints the crosses there to remind us that our paths will be similar to the one laid out for His Son. We, too, are recognized by His love given freely for others, marked for sacrifice in some way, empowered by worship and thanksgiving, and filled with His Spirit. This is real life, the abundant life, the only life I want.

Come to think of it, the stories I most love to tell unfolded on the back of one donkey or another. God has stopped me on my path countless times when I least expected it, when it was highly inconvenient. I've felt ashamed many times at my all-too-human responses to the things He allowed. But when I've bowed low, His presence has shown brightest. When my heart has been most empty, He has filled it with Himself. When my need has been greatest, He has spoken life-changing words through my donkeys; He has met me face-to-face. And I have never been the same after an encounter with the living God. Neither will you. That's wonderful news!

Face to Face

- Are there waves in your life that threaten you? What are they? What have you done to reach out for Jesus' strong arm of support? If doubts hold you back, confess them to God and ask Him to lift you up one day at a time.

- What will happen to the authenticity and sweetness of your walk with God if you elect to rebel in your spirit and not accept what He has allowed in your life? How might Joni's journey have been different had she not surrendered the outcome of her life to God? What verses encourage you to keep trusting Him today?

- Consider again Jesus' words in John 15:

> *"Live in me. Make your home in me just as I do in you. In the same way that a branch can't bear grapes by itself but only by being joined to the Vine, you can't bear fruit unless you are joined with me.*
>
> *"I am the Vine, you are the branches. When you're joined with me and I with you, the relation intimate and organic, the harvest is sure to be abundant. Separated, you can't produce a thing."* (MSG)

What strikes you most forcefully in Jesus' words? When you abide in the Vine, how does it change the way you feel about and respond to the donkeys in your life?

• What is your favorite story from one of your rides on a donkey? As you recall the memory of that leg of your journey, in what ways can you see that you were being guided and empowered by the Spirit within?

• Is Jesus really Lord of your life today? Have you asked Him to call the shots, to lead you and guide you every day through His Holy Spirit living in you? You can invite Him anytime, any day, to fill you with His Spirit and guide you from within. Write a prayer to Him thanking Him for guiding you on this journey and speaking to you intimately and powerfully in so many unexpected places.

Truth for the Surefooted Journey

Be joyful always; pray continually; give thanks in all circumstances, for this is God's will for you in Christ Jesus. (1 Thessalonians 5:16-18)

For in Christ all the fullness of the Deity lives in bodily form, and you have been given fullness in Christ, who is the head over every power and authority. (Colossians 2:9-10)

FINDING YOUR WAY HOME

HAVE YOU EVER been on a hike or a road trip and discovered you were lost? It can be pretty frightening, can't it? Life is much the same. Even if we've been out wandering around on the trail a long time, nothing feels more wonderful than finding the road home.

God's Word tells us that the only way to His Home is through His Son. Jesus said, "I am the way and the truth and the life. No one comes to the Father except through me" (John 14:6).

Receiving eternal life means putting our faith in Jesus' death on the cross as payment in full for our sins. It means agreeing with God that we've been headed down our own trail a long time. That's all sin is: doing life our way rather than God's way. And, Scripture tells us, "*All* have sinned and fall short of the glory of God" (Romans 3:23, emphasis added).

Like any gift, salvation must be received. Jesus will come into your life as the indwelling Holy Spirit when you invite Him in. When you do, you become a permanent and beloved member of God's own family. Here's a simple way to pray for salvation through Christ:

*Lord Jesus, please come into my heart today and for-
give my sins. I want to turn from my own way and follow You instead. Thank You for forgiving my sin and
for giving me Your Holy Spirit as my daily Guide.
Thank You for Your promise of eternal life. Please help
me live each day of my life to Your honor and glory.
Amen.*

Be assured that on your journey, God has plenty of good things planned for you, especially that you may know Him better day by day.

If you would like to contact me, I'd consider it a privilege to pray for you. You may do so via my websites: www.donkeysstilltalk.com or www.virellekidder.com. If you prefer, you may write to me at P.O. Box 246, Guilderland, NY 12084.

notes

CHAPTER 1
1. This section is the author's paraphrase of Numbers 22.
2. Portions of this chapter first appeared as "God Is Talking to You!" in *Today's Christian Woman* (January/February 2003).

CHAPTER 2
1. This section is the author's paraphrase of Genesis 37–45.
2. John Eldredge, *The Journey of Desire* (Nashville: Thomas Nelson, 2000), p. 61.

CHAPTER 3
1. Oswald Chambers, *My Utmost for His Highest* (New York: Dodd, Mead, 1935), p. 45.

CHAPTER 4
1. Oswald Chambers, *My Utmost for His Highest* (New York: Dodd, Mead, 1935), p. 173.
2. Judy Hampton, *Under the Circumstances* (Colorado Springs, Colo.: NavPress, 2001), p. 88.

CHAPTER 6
1. Cynthia Heald, *Abiding in Christ* (Colorado Springs, Colo.: NavPress, 1995), p. 38.

CHAPTER 7
1. This section is the author's paraphrase of 2 Kings 4.
2. Catherine Marshall, *Beyond Ourselves* (New York: Avon Books, 1961), p. 94.
3. Marshall, p. 91.

CHAPTER 8
1. This section is the author's paraphrase of Matthew 14:25-33.

ABOUT THE AUTHOR

FOR MORE THAN twenty years, Virelle Kidder has been in the saddle doing what she loves best: speaking to audiences around the country and abroad about the love of Christ. Virelle is a "people person" who relates instantly and warmly to audiences of all sizes. She is funny, transparent, highly relevant, and solidly biblical.

A former radio talk show host and now a full-time writer and conference speaker, Virelle spends a lot of her life encouraging others on their spiritual journeys. She is the author of three previous books: *Getting the Best Out of Public Schools* (coauthored with her husband, Steve, an educational psychologist); *Mothering Upstream*; and *Loving, Launching, and Letting Go*. *Donkeys Still Talk* is based on one of her most popular retreats.

Virelle is a contributing writer for *Today's Christian Woman* and is widely published in national print media. Her articles have been reprinted around the world. She and Steve have four grown children and five grandchildren and live in upstate New York.

You may write to Virelle or contact her for speaking through her websites, www.donkeysstilltalk.com or www.virellekidder.com, or by mail at P.O. Box 246, Guilderland, NY 12084.

Can't Get Enough? Check Out These Other Great Titles from NavPress!

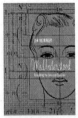

Ms. Understood
Jen Hatmaker
978-1-60006-216-2

Throughout history, it seems that women are defined by their culture: sometimes revered and sometimes shunned, almost always misunderstood. Author Jen Hatmaker invites women to flip the equation on the world's expectations for the fairer sex. Filled with her trademark wit and irrepressible enthusiasm, *Ms. Understood* inspires women to fearlessly pursue all that God has in store for their lives.

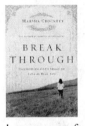

Break Through
Marsha Crockett
978-1-60006-185-1

Marsha Crockett knows the pain of a hard life. She invites you to search for the promise of God's power as you reconcile the reality of life with your faith. Through journal suggestions, Scripture meditation exercises, and practical tips, you'll learn how to move from stone-like hardness into a place of grace and truth.

Satisfy My Thirsty Soul
Linda Dillow
978-1-57683-390-2

As a Christian woman, you yearn for intimacy with God. You long to know His presence, to be satisfied in heart and soul, but you don't know how. You want to be obedient, but you need a higher motivation than simply choosing to do right. Linda Dillow understands. And now in *Satisfy My Thirsty Soul*, she shares with you her lifelong discovery that both longings can be met—through worship.

To order copies, call NavPress at 1-800-366-7788
or log on to www.navpress.com